BEHIND THE CAMERA

James Cameron

Ron Howard

Spike Lee

George Lucas

Rob Reiner

Steven Spielberg

Spike Lee

Charles J. Shields

Chelsea House Publishers
Philadelphia

Frontis: Spike Lee has emerged as one of Hollywood's most provocative filmmakers who is courting controversy today with films like *Bamboozled*.

CHELSEA HOUSE PUBLISHERS

EDITOR IN CHIEF Sally Cheney
DIRECTOR OF PRODUCTION Kim Shinners
CREATIVE MANAGER Takeshi Takahashi
MANUFACTURING MANAGER Diann Grasse

STAFF FOR SPIKE LEE

ASSOCIATE EDITOR Ben Kim
PRODUCTION ASSISTANT Jaimie Winkler
PICTURE RESEARCHER Sarah Bloom
SERIES AND COVER DESIGNER Takeshi Takahashi
LAYOUT 21st Century Publishing and Communications, Inc.

http://www.chelseahouse.com

First Printing

1 3 5 7 9 8 6 4 2

Library of Congress Cataloging-in-Publication Data

Shields, Charles J., 1951-
    Spike Lee / Charles J. Shields.
        p. cm.—(Behind the camera)
Includes bibliographical references and index.
    ISBN 0-7910-6715-7 (hardcover)
    1. Lee, Spike—Juvenile literature. 2. Motion picture producers and directors—
United States—Biography—Juvenile literature. I. Title. II. Series.
PN1998.3.L44 S45 2002
791.43'0233'092
                                                    2002003772

Table of Contents

1 Wake Up   7

2 Birth of a Director   17

3 Touching a Raw Nerve   33

4 Firebrand   43

5 "Malcolm-Mania"   51

6 Trial and Error   61

7 Spike vs. Everybody   75

8 Spike on Spike   85

   Chronology   90
   Filmography   91
   Major Awards   93
   Bibliography   94
   Further Reading   99
   Websites   100
   Index   101

Spike Lee has never shied away from challenging his audiences or his critics. His 2000 film *Bamboozled* is a biting satire about a minstrel show that becomes a top-rated TV program. The film was met by staunch protests, even before its release.

Chapter 1

Wake Up

Lee is a troublemaker, a valuable one.

—Stanley Kauffman,
film critic and Academy
Award-winning director

"PRAY TELL, NEGRO."

In Spike Lee's 2000 film, *Bamboozled*, Damon Wayans as Pierre Delacroix says "Pray tell, Negro" over and over in a phony, British-sounding accent until the remark begins to grate on the audience. But that's one of the smaller annoyances of the film. The entire movie got under the skin of both audiences and critics. Although *Bamboozled* is a bitter satire about how a minstrel show—a childish brand of clowning featuring blacks—could become the most popular program on television, audiences found themselves laughing guiltily.

"How is an audience supposed to react?" an interviewer from *Flick* magazine asked Lee.

"Aghast, shocked, startled, but laughing, because it is the number one show on television," replied Lee.

His answer might seem a little bewildering. Why would a director want an audience to feel conflicting emotions: laughing at African-American actors behaving like eye-rolling, joke-telling "darkies" from long ago, but feeling uncomfortable at the same time?

Because Lee wants audiences to think.

Spike Lee has directed 23 films, produced or executive-produced 19, has writer credit on 11, and is the author of numerous books aimed at "the demystification of film-making." He has lectured at Harvard University, New York University, and participated in numerous panels with some of the most forward-looking thinkers of the day.

And controversy has dogged him every step of the way. He raises issues, asks questions, and attacks popular notions relentlessly. He shakes audiences out of their normal feelings of detachment at watching a movie, and forces them to take a stand on what they've just seen.

The way studio executives reacted to his 1989 film *Do the Right Thing* was typical. Recalled Lee, "When the lights came up at the end of the screening, the studio brass just sat there in silence, almost stupefied. The silence went on for what seemed like an eternity. Finally

I asked Tom Pollock, president of Universal, 'So are we gonna get a release?' Everyone started to laugh, the ice had been broken."

As a result of his two-fisted approach to movie-making, Lee has earned a reputation. An interview with Lee posted by the website Cinequest begins: "Whether or not you like Spike Lee or have ever seen a Spike Lee film is irrelevant. You have an opinion of him as an individual and as a thinker. Over the course of Spike Lee's eclectic career, the media has created a persona of near mythic proportions— 'angry,' 'brilliant,' 'controversial'—but often left out is that he has become one of America's most talented, intelligent and prolific filmmakers."

Over the course of his career, Lee has treated on film a host of controversial topics—women's sexuality, racism, violence, drug-running, intolerance. As well as historically important events, too—the rise of Malcom X, the bombing of an all-black church in Birmingham in 1963, and the Million Man March in Washington, D.C. Each time, he focuses intensely on his subject, examining it not only through his eyes as director, but also through the characters' and the audiences', too. The effect is often "startling," as Lee himself says, but intimidating, too.

In a *Christian Science Monitor* film review of *Bamboozled* under the headline, "Spike Lee Shocks with Wild Race Tale," critic David Sterritt wrote, "A friend of mine once likened a Spike Lee movie to an overloaded truck. It's piled too high, it's going too fast, it tilts precariously as it speeds around the bends, and sometimes it hops the curb and sends pedestrians running for their lives. But it's exciting to watch, your eyes are riveted to its every move, and you have to admit you've never seen anything like it."

Bamboozled is a perfect example of Lee's delight in shaking things up. He turns his cameras to the entertainment industry itself, and how African-American performers can be seduced into humiliating themselves for mainstream audiences.

"The goal of this film," said Lee, "was to put the focus back on the media and its misuses and abuses of people, as well as the people that get co-opted, who go along and fall for the okey-doke."

In the film, a television network chief orders Wayans as Pierre Delacroix to deliver a show as black as the mid-1950s television show, "Amos 'n' Andy." Delacroix decides to sabotage the project by producing the most monumental racial throwback he can think of—"Mantan: The New Millennium Minstrel Show," starring tap-dance wonder Savion Glover and comic veteran Tommy Davidson as a pair of prancing plantation darkies named Mantan and Sleep 'N' Eat. An enthusiastic sponsor is lined up: a malt liquor called Da Bomb (it comes in a bomb-shaped bottle with fins). Commercials for it feature rappers urging viewers to "get your freak on." Delacroix is certain the show will be such an outrage that he'll be fired, and Americans' consciences will be shaken-up.

Instead, "Mantan" becomes a hit.

White people, delighted by the antics they see, get a laugh everywhere by repeating the show's catch-phrase, "I's a nigger!" Near the end of the film, Delacroix contemplates a remark by black author James Baldwin, "People pay for what they do, and even more for what they have become." On the other hand, Delacroix also remembers the advice of his father, a statement that seems to be the code of the entertainment industry, "Leave 'em laughing." As Lee likes to do, he leaves his audience to figure out for

Bamboozled forced audiences of all races to acknowledge and confront the racial stereotypes and images that have affected our entertainment industry. Despite the controversy surrounding the film, it also earned praise as an uncompromising satire from a talented director.

themselves which piece of philosophy they believe.

Even before the film had appeared on theater screens, however, *Bamboozled* drew howls of protest.

The *New York Times* refused to run an ad for the movie showing a "pickininny"—a black child with a headful of pigtails and ribbons—grinning at a slice of watermelon. Even the posters themselves—a caricature with a black face and excessively large, bright red lips—were viewed as objectionable by theater-owners. Other advertisements showed the faces of the film's African-American actors daubed with burnt cork historically known as "blackface."

Lee remained unmoved. "I did not make up blackface. I acknowledge that it is offensive to some people," he said. "But, just because it is offensive, that does not negate the fact that we still need to deal with these images." As part of his research into the links between racism and entertainment, Lee purchased black memorabilia items, including "mammy," "sambo," and "Aunt Jemima" dolls, and other accessories such as the "Jolly Nigger" bank, featured in *Bamboozled*. He also viewed clips from movies and television where blackface had been employed as a comic device. One of his favorite cartoons even surprised him. "I had never seen Bugs Bunny in blackface before," he said.

Moreover, he hoped that people's temporary shock would turn into a discussion of a problem he wanted to explore: black exploitation by the entertainment industry. "I think this film raises the stakes for African American performers. It might put them under scrutiny . . . Maybe audiences will start to wonder about the roles they play and the songs they sing." As examples, in interviews Lee pointed to two TV programs he objected to, accusing them of demeaning blacks: "The Secret Diary of Desmond

Pfeiffer" which aired for a short time on UPN, and "Homeboys from Outer Space" which ran on WB.

But *Bamboozled* also drew praise, too, primarily for Lee's courage. Wrote media critic Andrew Thompson:

> Spike Lee's unflinching take on America's ingrained pastime of racism has often made him a scapegoat for media critics—white, black and all shades in between. With his new DV [digital video] feature *Bamboozled*, the writer/director strikes back, pointing his finger at an entertainment industry that loves to categorize African-Americans as its cultural court jesters. While the doo-rag wearing mammy, the oversexed big buck and faithful ol' Uncle Tom represent the most damning of African-American stereotypes, it's the "coon"—that ever-chipper, bug-eyed, teeth-grinning icon—that Lee takes to task here. This social satire is right on time too, as Lee's lambasting of television comes hot-on-the-heels of the recent blasting of a virtually whitewashed TV wasteland by a Kwesi Mfume-led NAACP [National Association of Colored People].

Lee styles himself the enemy of the "gatekeepers," as he calls them: "The gatekeepers—these are the people that decide what goes on television, what movies are made, what gets heard on the radio, what's getting written in the magazines—I can tell you those are all exclusively white males. These are the guys making the choices for all of Western Civilization. There are seven or eight guys, and they decide, boom, this is what we're gonna do. And we've got to get in those positions. And that's when you'll start to see some change."

Fighting against the gatekeepers, Lee positions himself as a gatecrasher: an independent filmmaker who examines tough problems in American society by using his

THE FORUM
INSTITUTE OF POLITICS

In his films and in frequent lectures (like this one at Harvard),
Lee openly characterizes himself as a gatecrasher—challenging
the limits of censorship, artistic expression, and social standards.

camera like a stun gun. "Wake up" is his message, and
one of his favorite visual reminders of this theme is a
clock. In *Bamboozled*, a clock appears prominently in the
home of the sellout character, Pierre Delacroix.

"Lee is a troublemaker, a valuable one," wrote film critic
and Academy Award-winning director Stanley Kauffman in

the pages of the *New Republic* magazine. "He can talk loosely and can make flat or forced films; he can also make pungent, large, authentic works such as *Do the Right Thing* and *Malcolm X*. *Bamboozled* is less organically sound than either of those pictures, but it is an important contribution, I hope, to American discomfort."

The title for *Bamboozled* comes from a speech by Malcolm X. In this speech, Malcolm X urged blacks in the United States to realize that the American Dream had not been intended for them. "You've been hoodwinked. You've been had. You've been took. You've been led astray, run amok," he said. "You've been bamboozled." In many ways, this warning becomes a theme in Spike Lee's movies. Contributing to American discomfort—that might make a fitting artistic motto for Spike Lee, the most prominent and influential black filmmaker today.

Growing up in the Fort Greene section of Brooklyn, a young Spike Lee was surrounded by New York's rich musical culture. The area was known as a gathering place for jazz musicians, and Spike's father Bill was himself an accomplished jazz bassist and composer.

Chapter 2

Birth of a Director

Growing up in this country, the rich culture I saw in my neighborhood, in my family, I didn't see that on television or on the movie screen. It was always my ambition that if I was successful I would try to portray a truthful portrait of African-Americans in this country, negative and positive.

—Spike Lee

FORT GREENE, WHERE Spike Lee grew up, is a small neighborhood is northern Brooklyn about a 15-minute walk from the Brooklyn Bridge. Brooklyn is one of five boroughs of New York City. With an area roughly 73 square miles in size, and a population of over 2.3 million, Brooklyn has the largest number of homes in the city. Although Lee was born in Atlanta, Georgia on March 20, 1957 his family moved to New York City when he was still a toddler. Eventually, there would be five children in the family: Shelton, later nicknamed "Spike" for his toughness by his mother; younger brothers Chris and David, born in 1958 and 1960 respectively; sister Joie, born in 1963; and brother Cinque, born in 1968.

For a family whose interests and income were tied to the arts, New York City was the place to be in the early 1960s. Spike's father, Bill Lee, a jazz bass player and composer called "Bleek" by his friends, was riding the folk music movement to the top by accompanying singer Odetta. Said a reviewer of a reissued collection of Odetta's music several years ago, "Like Sweet Honey in the Rock and the late Paul Robeson, Odetta booms out centuries of black oppression and injustice. Yet deep dignity is a cornerstone of her art. With only bassist Bill Lee (father of Spike) to accompany her powerful voice and acoustic guitar, this heavily traditional reissue presents the early-'60s folk boom at its best: passionate performance, arresting songs, and the immaculate Vanguard [recording label] sound."

The Fort Greene neighborhood had a reputation as a community where musicians could find a bed for a night, or meet-up with fellow performers, like minstrels traveling from city to city. Live music could be heard pouring from an open window on summer nights. Jazz trombonist Slide Hampton remembered, "We had 13, 14 rooms in the house, right in Fort Greene, right around the corner from Spike Lee's father, Bill Lee. A lot of musicians lived in that area. There were jam sessions and people practicing and rehearsing for years."

Music could be heard coming from the Lee home, too. Bill Lee was often in demand, playing with, besides Odetta, Chick Corea or Aretha Franklin, for instance. On the other hand, a musician's income is not usually steady. In Spike Lee's semi-autobiographical 1994 film, *Crooklyn*, the family struggles in genteel poverty because the musician father's gigs come in spurts. Nevertheless, Spike's father tried to inspire his children with African-American jazz, hoping a love of it might catch on. Records by Miles Davis, John Coltrane, Charles Mingus, Art Blakely, Thelonious Monk and others played in the background of the Lee home as a constant theme.

Also while the children were growing up, Spike's mother Jacqueline, a teacher, encouraged their appreciation of black art and literature. "I was forced to read [poet] Langston Hughes, that kind of stuff," Lee told *Vanity Fair.* "And I'm glad my mother made me do that." When he was old enough, Spike was enrolled at St. Ann's, one of the city's most highly regarded private schools where his mother taught. But later he insisted on switching to the local public school instead, so he could be with black friends. The choice divided his world from his siblings'. "Spike used to point out the differences in our friends," recalled his sister Joie, who was a private school student. "By the time I was a senior," she told *Mother Jones,* "I was being channeled into white colleges."

But despite his parents' influence, Spike was not drawn to the arts. "I remember going to see Broadway plays, 'The King and I,' stuff like that. Now I could see that that exposure was very important, even though I didn't know that that was what I wanted to do, even though I didn't want to see these plays, I did not want to see my father play jazz." He went to movies with friends—mainly to horse around, not because the big screen fascinated him. "[We] sat through the film six times every Saturday and drank all the Coca Cola we could drink and ate all the popcorn we could eat and threw stuff at the screen and tried not to get thrown out." If anyone asked what he wanted to do when he grew up, he had his answer ready. He was going to play second base for the Mets. But "genetics conspired against that dream happening," he later joked.

The only thing that really appealed to him was something hard to put his finger on. It had to do with watching the unrehearsed drama of life all around him. Listening to the belligerent talk of his Italian classmates at school; overhearing stories told in mom-and-pop stores; registering in his subconscious the shouts, laughter, and sometimes racial taunts heard at Coney Island beach; watching homeless people asking for spare change on subway platforms. He barely needed to venture outside his own neighborhood to see how life had affected people differently. In the 1960s Fort Greene was going through a long economic decline, and Lee saw a "vast spectrum—people making it, people struggling to make it, people in between. I'm very observant. For the most part, I don't even talk; I just watch and listen to people."

But none of this was leading him in a clear direction, at least when it came to a career. So after graduating from John Dewey High School in 1975, he enrolled in his father and grandfather's alma mater—the all-male, historically black Morehouse College in Atlanta,

Georgia. At least he would be guaranteed a top-flight liberal arts education, besides the chance to have future African-American leaders in business, medicine, science, and the arts as college classmates.

Morehouse College, named in honor of Henry L. Morehouse, the corresponding secretary of the Atlanta Baptist Home Mission Society, is a remarkable institution. It was founded in 1867 as Augusta Institute by the Rev. William Jefferson White, a Baptist minister and cabinetmaker, with the support of Richard C. Coulter, a former slave, and the Rev. Edmund Turney, organizer of the National Theological Institute for educating freedmen in Washington, D.C. The site selected for the campus was where Confederate soldiers mounted a last-ditch, determined resistance to Union forces during the siege of Atlanta. Directly across from Morehouse is Spelman College, another historically black selective college for women only, which gradually became a leading institution as well.

Today, Morehouse delivers, in the words of its administration, "an exceptional educational experience that today meets the intellectual, moral, and spiritual needs of students representing more than 40 states and 18 countries—a unique institution dedicated, as always, to producing outstanding men and extraordinary leaders to serve God and humanity." Among its graduates, Morehouse counts Robert E. Johnson '48, former executive editor and associate publisher of *Jet* magazine; Martin Luther King Jr. '48, Nobel Peace Prize laureate and civil rights leader; Don Clendenon '56 New York Mets outfielder and 1969 World Series MVP; Edwin C. Moses '78 Olympic gold medalist and financial consultant for Robinson-Humphrey Co. Inc.; James M. Nabrit '23,

Although Lee had at one time wanted to play pro baseball, he instead enrolled at his father's alma mater, the historically black Morehouse College in Atlanta. Along with Spelman—Atlanta's black women's college—Morehouse provides educational opportunities for the next generation of African-American leaders in business, science, and the arts.

former U.S. ambassador to the United Nations and former president of Howard University; Maynard H. Jackson '56 chairman and CEO of Jackson Securities Inc. and first African-American mayor of Atlanta; and Samuel L. Jackson '72; Academy Award nominee and motion picture actor.

Like most newcomers to college, Lee would have eventually found his way into a major field of study at Morehouse. Maybe a particular class would have sparked his interest, or a special professor would have taken him under his wing. But in 1977, when Spike was 20, something else happened that indirectly led to his life's work—his mother died of breast cancer.

Distraught by her death, Lee found it hard to shake off his grief, much less concentrate on his studies. To cheer him up, friends began inviting him to movies. Suddenly, films grabbed his interest like nothing else had. He became a fan of directors Bernardo Bertolucci, Martin Scorsese, and Akira Kurosawa, famous for their studies of character and human nature. When he saw Michael Cimino's *The Deer Hunter*, he told his friend John Wilson on the ride home, "John, I know what I want to do. I want to make films."

But his subject matter would the black experience in the United States, slices from the life that had fascinated him as a youngster in Fort Greene. "Growing up in this country, the rich culture I saw in my neighborhood, in my family, I didn't see that on television or on the movie screen," he told a San Francisco audience at the Imagination Conference in 1996. "It was always my ambition that if I was successful I would try to portray a truthful portrait of African-Americans in this country, negative and positive."

During summer of 1977—nicknamed the "Summer of Sam" by New Yorkers because of the serial killings committed by David Berkowitz under the alias "Sam"— Spike went around city shooting Super 8-mm film with a camera he purchased, trying to capture the feel of the times. He titled the edited version *Last Hustle in Brooklyn*, "which was really like a highlight film of black people and Puerto Rican people looting and dancing," he told the San Francisco audience in 1996. "When school began I showed it to my class and I got a favorable response and that's a great feeling, the initial time that happens, where you do something and people respond to it."

Morehouse didn't offer a degree in film studies, however, so Spike graduated in the field closest to it— mass communication. But he realized that he was not ready to be a filmmaker just because he liked films and had a college degree. At Morehouse, "We only had the facilities for Super 8, so I wanted to learn film grammar, learn how to make a film." He applied to the top three graduate programs in filmmaking in the country—the University of Southern California (USC); the University of California at Los Angeles (UCLA); and New York University (NYU). USC and UCLA required high scores on the Graduate Record Exam, and Spike's were modest, a fact he attributes to cultural bias on the tests. But NYU asked for portfolio of creative work. He submitted one and was accepted in NYU's Insitute of Film and Television Tisch School of Arts graduate film program.

Enrolling in film school—one that was located in New York City—blended his creative interests with his favorite environment. The center of NYU is its Washington Square campus in the heart of Greenwich Village, a historic neighborhood that has attracted generations of writers, musicians, artists, and intellectuals. For film students at NYU today, state-of-the-art facilities include 60 editing rooms, 25 film and video screening rooms and theaters, animation studios, a cinema studies archive, broadcast-quality television studios, and three film soundstages. Director Ang Lee delivered *Crouching Dragon, Hidden Tiger* only six years after graduating from Tisch School of the Arts.

Spike was one of about 50 students selected for the three-year program out of 800 applicants. In addition to his talent, he brought something else to the classroom, too—he was black, one of only a few enrolled. It wasn't long before his perspective clashed with his instructors'. The flashpoint was D.W. Griffith's highly controversial 1915 film, *Birth of a Nation*.

Birth of a Nation is a silent film based on Rev. Thomas Dixon Jr.'s racist play, *The Clansman*, and incredibly, the film is still used today as a recruitment piece for Klu Klux Klan (KKK) membership. Its presentation of the KKK as heroes and Southern blacks as villains after the Civil War appealed to white Americans' nostalgia for the Old South. The film's major black roles—all of them stereotypes—were played by white actors in blackface. In the film's climactic finale, blacks are "put back in their place," calming white Americans' fears the rise of defiant, determined, and sexually powerful black men. Southern-born president Woodrow Wilson is reported to have exclaimed during a private screening at the White House, "It's like writing history with lightning. And my only regret is that it is all terribly truc." The National Association of Colored People (NAACP) denounced the film as "the meanest vilification of the Negro race." Riots broke out in major cities, and lawsuits and picketing outside theaters made the film notorious.

Today, *Birth of a Nation* is shown in film schools for the sake of scholarship. To expose students to the impact of an historic piece of art in the early days of filmmaking,

As a student at NYU's film school, Spike found controversy early. In a rebuttal to D.W. Griffith's film, *Birth of a Nation*—in which the Ku Klux Klan is portrayed heroically—Lee submitted *The Answer*, a ten-minute short film that was panned by students and that nearly resulted in Lee's expulsion.

and to point out the film's cinematic innovations—dolly shots, crane shots, special effects, even a color sequence at the end.

Watching the film in class, Spike could appreciate the historical reasons for showing it, but he vehemently objected to the professor's failure to mention that dozens of blacks were lynched by mobs inspired by the film. For his first-year project, he wrote and directed a ten-minute short, *The Answer*, in which a black screenwriter is assigned to rewrite *Birth of a Nation*. Not only did student critics pan it, but some of NYU's instructors were offended. Lee later told *Mother Jones* magazine, "I was told I was whiskers from being kicked out."

Chastened maybe, but undiscouraged, he took heart from what had been accomplished by a classmate, Jim Jarmusch. Jarmusch's first year out of NYU saw the release of his feature-length film, *Stranger than Paradise*. The effect on Spike was electric. "Here was someone I knew, someone who went to the same school that I did, who now had a hit film," Lee told *Indienetwork.com*. "I worked in the equipment room as a TA [teaching assistant] and I had checked equipment out to him, and here was someone who had an international hit. To me, that's when it first became do-able. . . . He showed me and everyone at NYU that we could do this."

For his student thesis—a major project required for his master's degree—Lee directed *Joe's Bed-Stuy Barbershop: We Cut Heads*, a 60-minute film that recreates the world of the corner barbershop, the local meeting place where people talk, put nickels and dimes on their lucky numbers and the dream of making the big "hit." When *Bed-Stuy* made the rounds on campus, classmates and instructors were so impressed that Lee was suddenly talked about as one of the most promising young filmmakers at NYU. The year after his graduation in 1983, *Bed-Stuy* won the Motion Picture Arts and Sciences' Student Academy Award.

An agent from the William Morris agency, one of the premier creative talent agencies in the country, offered to represent him. He told the starry-eyed young director, "Look Spike, just leave everything up to me, I know how to handle the studios. Just sit back and wait by the phone." Dutifully, Lee waited, his Motion Picture Arts and Sciences plaque propped-up on a TV until, "Ma Bell turned the phone off. And then Brooklyn Union Gas followed shortly thereafter."

Lee felt certain that racism in the entertainment industry had just taken its first swipe at him. If he was going to make a full-length film, he decided, he was going to have to do it as an independent filmmaker. That meant writing the script, raising the money, directing the film, supervising the editing, and finding a studio to get behind the release.

It was much harder than he ever had imagined.

He wrote a script called *The Messenger* about a bike messenger. Then, "I got involved with some bogus producer who said he was going to deliver on the financing of the film," he continued in his speech to the San Francisco audience. Excited, he enlisted help from fellow classmates to serve as cast and crew members. For 12 days in the summer of 1984, they shot the entire film. And then Lee waited for a wire transfer of the money to his production account. It never came. Angry and humiliated, he had to assemble everyone and explain that the film they had worked on was never going to be made. Worse, he had no money to pay them.

Not long after, Lee said, "I was crying like a baby sitting in my bathtub. All the water had drained out. I was wrinkled like a California raisin and I was ready to quit. I said 'Well, let me give it one more try. I'm going to pick myself up off the canvas and try it once again. Just try to re-evaluate where I went wrong.'" He had to admit he had made a fundamental error—the project had been too big and too ambitious. He needed to think what he could pull off well on a small budget: fewer actors, simpler shots, maybe even shooting in Super 16 black-and-white and having it blown-up to 35mm.

While working for a film distribution company, Lee raised the financing he needed. His family pitched in too, bringing the total to $175,000. Exactly a year after the disaster of *The Messenger*, Lee began shooting *She's Gotta Have It* with rented equipment. The set was his own apartment. *She's Gotta Have It* is the satirical story of Nola Darling, a black woman who uninhibitedly enjoys sex with her three lovers. Lee took the part of Mars Blackmon, making popular the line, "Please baby, please baby, please baby, baby, baby, please." Near the film's end, Nola invites all three men to a Thanksgiving Day dinner, creating a funny and unsettling situation. Shooting took 12 days. By the time the film wrapped, Lee was so strapped for cash that the film's processing lab threatened to auction off the negative.

Island Pictures agreed to distribute the film, and in 1986, the year of its release, *She's Gotta Have It* earned the coveted young filmmaker's award, the Prix de Jeunesse Award at the Cannes Film Festival. Audiences packed theaters to see the film—not only black audiences, but crossover movie-goers who liked the film's offbeat style. Box office ticket sales topped $8 million.

With his share of the profits, Spike endowed a film-making program at Brooklyn's Long Island University

After some initial setbacks, Spike Lee burst onto the public scene in 1986 with the release of *She's Gotta Have It*. Shot in 12 days for a budget of $175,000, the film earned the prestigious Prix de Jeunesse Ward at the Cannes Film Festival. Here the cast (and Spike Lee in hat and glasses) poses for a publicity shot.

to teach others about cinematic art. He called it Forty Acres and a Mule Institute—a reference to the federal government's broken promise after the Civil War to pay that amount to slaves in reparation. In Fort Greene, his old neighborhood, he opened Forty Acres and a Mule

Filmmaking, his own independent film company.

There had been a time when Spike Lee had gone to the movies on Saturdays to throw popcorn at the screen. After the success of *She's Gotta Have It*, he was talked about as a leader in the Black New Wave in American cinema.

Now that Lee had grabbed Hollywood's attention, he had no intention of letting go. In *Do the Right Thing*, he takes an unblinking look at urban race relations with his native Brooklyn as the backdrop.

Chapter 3

Touching a Raw Nerve

Essentially what I hoped was that [Do the Right Thing] *would provoke everybody, white and black.*

—Spike Lee

FOLLOWING THE SUCCESS of *She's Gotta Have It*, Hollywood opened its door to Spike Lee, and producers opened their wallets. Never one to pass by a chance to stir up audiences, however, Lee chose not to take the easy the way. He could have opted for a safe topic or script, one that would have feathered his nest, professionally and financially. Instead, he went headlong at an unpleasant subject—racism. And not between whites and blacks, either, but mainly among blacks. In addition, he chose his undergraduate alma mater for the movie's setting: Morehouse College in Atlanta.

The theme was color discrimination—lighter skin versus darker skin. "The people with the money, " he told the *New York Times,* "most of them have light skin. They have the Porsches, the B.M.W.'s, the quote good hair unquote. The others, the kids from the rural south, have bad, kinky hair. When I was in school, we saw all this going on." By focusing on a black college campus, he told *Newsweek* magazine, he could expose in miniature painful issues that many African-Americans, he argued, did not want to address.

But audiences would hardly be drawn to anything that was so provoking. On the other hand, *She's Gotta Have It* had done well at the box office, despite its edgy subject—a carefree woman shares three male lovers— in part because it was funny. So as Lee crafted his second major feature, *School Daze* (1988), he injected musical comedy to leaven the story. Just like the summer of 1977, when he filmed "looting and dancing" in the streets of New York with a Super 8 camera, Lee decided to use music, dancing, and humor for contrast in treating racism, a serious subject. The method would later become part of his trademark directorial style in many of his films.

For *School Daze*, Lee continued using what he called "guerilla filmmaking" techniques: using a low-budget approach and a committed crew to stay under the radar—beneath the notice—of studio executives who might try to squash the project. He cast himself in a role, as he would in many of his films, alongside Laurence Fishburne and Giancarlo Esposito. In the storyline, "gamma" girls in the college's sorority system make themselves look like white beauty queens, which gets the approval of their snobbish boyfriends. As a clique, these social wannabes look down on Afrocentric "niggers," black classmates who don't come up to their standards. While this might sound like the kind of meanness that can happen in a high school much less a college, Lee was proposing that a more serious issue was just under the surface—black self-hatred. Through satire, Lee meant to expose the cruelty of young black people accepting and practicing white-encouraged racism.

To cover production costs, Island Pictures allotted Lee with about one-third the budget normally given to feature-length movies. But when the tab reached $4 million and the film still wasn't finished, the studio pulled out. Having been burned this way once before on his first film, *The Messenger*, Lee went directly to another studio, Columbia Pictures. Within two days, he had hammered down a deal that netted him $2 million more for production. But studio heads at Columbia apparently misread what *School Daze* was about. "They saw music, they saw dancing, they saw comedy," Lee told *Mother Jones* magazine. When the real nature of the film emerged during a screening for Columbia executives, they quietly put the brakes on. *School Daze* received faint promotion and poor distribution. Nevertheless, it netted $15 million at the box office—nearly twice the amount spent to make it.

As Lee no doubt hoped, the black community responded harshly to *School Daze*. He was accused of airing dirty

As the inspiration for *School Daze*, Lee returned to his experiences at Morehouse College. Rather than examining race relations between blacks and whites, the film addresses the complex social dynamics among African-Americans at a single university.

laundry about black identity and separatism. In addition, he had even questioned whether a traditional college education led African-Americans in the right direction, and for this he was chastised, too. But "*School Daze* bored white audiences," said cultural critic Alan Stone in the *Boston Review*, "in part because Lee had no real interest in saying anything to them." Moreover, Stone claimed, the film was "stylistically confused"—the struggle for black identity interrupted by old-fashioned Hollywood dance numbers. "Lee's directorial penchant for the weird is much in evidence," he complained.

But Lee had strongly introduced one of his major themes: the urgency of lifting the weight of white oppression, in many forms, off the shoulders of blacks. To his mind, this was critical. And in his next film, *Do the Right Thing*, he would deliver that message with the force of cannon-fire.

In 1986, Lee read news accounts about an incident in Howard Beach, a New York neighborhood, where white youths attacked three black men. One of the victims, Michael Griffith, tried to run across a busy street and was struck and killed by a passing car. The story provided Lee with the germ of an idea. But rather than stick to the facts, he decided to expand on the event because, as he explained to the *New York Times*, "There's more opportunity in fiction."

In *Do the Right Thing*, released in 1989, the setting is the hottest day of the year in Bedford-Stuyvesant with tempers frayed to the breaking point. Then an episode of police brutality sets off an explosion of black racial revenge. Lee cast himself as Mookie who, as a pizza delivery man, serves as mediator between Sal, an Italian owner of a pizza parlor and his two sons on one side; and on the other, the black community living in the neighborhood. There are people like Buggin Out, a street hipster who expresses outrage that Sal's Famous Pizzeria's Wall of Fame contains only photographs of Italian show business and sports stars. There is Radio Raheem, whose massive boom box creates a world of sound around him, insulating him from other people.

On the sidelines, three sidewalk philosophers comment like a Greek chorus about the injustice of life, but lapse into high-spirited teasing. Smiley, a stutterer, sells copies of a photograph showing the Rev. Dr. Martin Luther King Jr. with Malcolm X, as if to suggest that to achieve social change, the middle way is best. To ensure that Sal did not become a white man effigy for the film's anger, Lee gave actor Danny Aiello the chance to improvise his part. The result is that Sal is a real person, one with whom white audiences can identity, and his relationship with Mookie resembles the bond between father and son.

From the first moments of the film, Lee plunges the audience into a kind of city symphony. Throughout the action, he weaves verbal and visual references to black culture, backgrounded by a musical score written by his father, jazz bassist Bill Lee. Now and then, like a fist, rap music punches through the soundtrack. In what Lee called a "racial slur montage"—each of Bedford-Stuyvesant's diverse racial representatives—Korean, Italian, black, etc.—sings a rap song lyric loaded with gleeful but shocking bigotry. The sweltering heat creates the sense that the neighborhood is a pressure cooker at full boil.

When white police officers kill a black man, the lid literally blows off. Mookie discards his role as peace-broker and hurls a garbage can through the window of the pizzeria, "to convey the suffering and final defeat of a rational man by an irrational world," said Murray Kempton in the *New York Review of Books*. A riot ensues, leaving the tension unresolved. The film ends with two opposing quotes on the screen, taunting the audience to take a stand: Martin Luther King's "The old law of an eye for an eye leaves everyone blind,"

The stunning climax of *Do the Right Thing* sparked controversy inside and outside the film world. Fearing the film would spur audiences to violence, critics accused Lee of exaggerating black anger to make the film's point. Despite the controversy, audiences made the film a huge success for Lee, earning him two Oscar nominations.

followed by Malcolm X's "I am not against violence in self-defense. I don't even call it violence when it's self-defense. I call it intelligence."

When word got out about the film and its violent climax, critics accused Lee of exaggerating black anger and wanting to stir up trouble. *New York* magazine warned, "Lee appears to be endorsing the outcome, and if some audiences go wild he's partly responsible." Lee responded in the pages of *People* magazine, "Black America is tired of having their brothers and sisters murdered by the police for no reason other than being black. I'm not advocating violence. I'm saying I can understand it. If the people are frustrated and feel oppressed and feel this is the only way they can act, I understand."

Audiences filled theaters to make up their own minds after *Do the Right Thing* became the subject of editorials, talk shows, and magazine articles. (Sociology courses in many colleges continue to show it as part of discussions about racism.) It became Lee's second-highest grossing film after *Malcolm X* and was honored with two Oscar nominations for Best Original Screenplay and Best Director. It also received the Los Angeles Film Critics Association's Best Director award.

"But what is clear enough now is that Mr. Lee, a bold, 32-year-old Brooklyn native, has with this film ventured into an area of film making that has touched a raw nerve," wrote the *New York Times* in June 1989.

"Essentially what I hoped was that it would provoke everybody, white and black," Lee said in the article. "I wanted to generate discussion about racism because too many people have their head in the sand about racism. They feel that the problem was eradicated in the 60's when Lyndon Johnson signed a few documents. For many white people, there is a view that black people have the vote and they can live next door to us and it's all done with and there's no more racism. As far as I'm concerned, racism is the most pressing problem in the United States; and I wanted the film to bring the issue into the forefront where it belongs."

The interviewer asked Lee whether he had indeed done the right thing considering the outcry the film had provoked.

"I'm sure I did," Lee answered. "And I think history will prove that."

Following *Do the Right Thing*, Lee continued his commentaries on race relations, both on and off screen. Several controversial interviews, coupled with the release of films like *Jungle Fever*, combined to enhance his image as an outspoken social critic.

Chapter 4

Firebrand

I give interracial couples a look. Daggers. They get uncomfortable when they see me on the street.

—Spike Lee

DO THE RIGHT THING put Spike Lee on the celebrity map, so to speak, not only as a filmmaker, but also as a social critic and role model. Because of his visibility, young directors such as John Singleton (*Boyz N the Hood*, 1991) and Matty Rich (*Straight Out of Brooklyn*, 1991) began receiving the financial support from Hollywood studios that had ignored Lee only a few years earlier. Interviewers from newspapers, magazines, and television eagerly descended on Spike, who could be counted on to speak his mind about race relations, politics, other filmmakers, and even basketball.

Sometimes, the results were unfortunate.

In October 1992, *Esquire* magazine ran an interview with Lee. The cover of the magazine trumpeted, "Spike Lee Hates Your Cracker Ass." Maybe feeling his oats as firebrand director, Lee had given forth with such ill-considered remarks as, "I give interracial couples a look. Daggers. They get uncomfortable when they see me on the street." He also recounted an incident that supposedly happened on the Oprah Winfrey Show. "[Liz] Claiborne got on and said she didn't make clothes for black people to wear. Oprah stopped the show and told her to get her ass off the set. How you gonna get on Oprah's show and say you don't make clothes for black women? It definitely happened . . . . Every black woman in America needs to go to her closet, throw that [expletive] out, and never buy another stitch of clothes from Claiborne."

The Claiborne-Winfrey "feud" never happened, as a matter of fact. Lee had repeated an urban legend he'd heard, and public relations people from the *Oprah Winfrey Show* rushed to do damage control by explaining that Liz Claiborne had never been on the program. She had retired as head of her company two years earlier.

Four years later in 1996, Lee was still getting grief about the article. "I get people coming to me in ball parks or on the street and asking me why I got to make it worse between the races," Lee told a reporter for *The Daily Bruin*, the campus newspaper of the University of California at Los Angeles. "Now, they may not be people who have

Mo' Better Blues examines a black musician's complex relationships and search for identity. With a jazz score written by his father Bill, Spike returned again to his Brooklyn roots. Despite an excellent performance by Denzel Washington, the film was criticized as being overly sentimental.

necessarily seen my movies, but who have walked by the newsstand in the airport, and seen my face on the cover of *Esquire* with the header 'Spike Lee hates your cracker-ass,' which I never ever said, just to sell more copies."

In the meantime, however, he had directed and released two films—*Mo' Better Blues* (1990) and *Jungle Fever* (1991)—that drew heated objections from critics, adding to his notoriety. He was accused of being intolerant, a charge he usually laid at the feet of others.

Mo' Better Blues marked the first time Lee worked with actor Denzel Washington, who later carried the lead in Lee's sixth film, *Malcolm X* (1992). Washington portrays

Bleek (his father's nickname) Gilliam, a self-absorbed jazz trumpeter forced to become sensitive to the needs others. "*Mo' Better Blues* is about relationships," Lee explained to *Ebony.* "It's not only about man-woman relationships, but about relationships in general—Bleek's relationship to his father and his manager, and his relationship with two female friends. Bleek's true love is music, and he is trying to find the right balance." Made in collaboration with Lee's father, who scored the music, *Mo' Better Blues* again featured show-biz style singing and dancing set against serious themes. In a sense, it was a musical celebration of black consciousness, black identity, and the need for black solidarity. Artistically, it was filled with Lee's characteristic energy, including a dolly shot that created the effect of actors moving effortlessly through space. But reviewers generally found the story sugary and nostalgic.

In any case, the recognition for its better points that the film deserved became lost in controversy. Lee's portrayal of whites was strongly criticized. In particular, the characters Moe and Josh Flatbush, the Jewish owners of the nightclub in the movie, raised cries of anti-Semitism. Writing in the *Boston Review*, Alan Stone suggested that Lee was attempting to turn the tables on white audiences, after decades of blacks appearing as stereotypes in movies, but the result was unworthy of him, he argued. "Lee gets into artistic trouble with his stereotypes not because they are cruel and demeaning but because they are weird, and this is typically the case with his depiction of whites. Weird caricature can be funny and interesting but it also turns the person into a thing, makes the subject into an object." On the practical side, Stone pointed out, offending white moviegoers was carrying a financial cost, too: "he has been turning off the cross-over audiences he

1991 saw the release of *Jungle Fever*, Spike Lee's look at the sexual affair between a married black professional and his working-class white secretary. The film challenged many taboos, and was met with the expected round of harsh criticism.

needs at the box office if he wants to make big movies."

Regardless, the following year, Lee released *Jungle Fever* (1991), a film with a storyline guaranteed to create controversy: a graphically sexual affair between a black married professional man Flipper Purify (Wesley Snipes) and his Italian-American working-class secretary, Angie (Annabella Sciorra). The inspiration for the film was the 1989 killing of Yusuf Hawkins, a young black man, by baseball bat-wielding Italian-American youths from the New York neighborhood of Bensonhurst. Hawkins was thought to have been dating a white woman. "I'm not saying all ethnic conflicts are between Italians and blacks, but the most violent ones, in my estimation, have been," Lee told the Los Angeles Times.

A reviewer for the magazine *L'Italio-Americano* found Lee's depiction of Italian-Americans offensive. "Lee portrays his New York Italian-American men as either gluttonous, violent animals or as overblown sentimental buffoons with a penchant for excessive emotionality. Angie's widowed father's appetite and bad table manners are exceeded only by his uncontrollable temper and violence. When he learns that she has taken up with Flipper, he beats her savagely . . . "

Lee explained that his purpose was to show how interracial relationships can be expressions of stereotyping—the attraction of the forbidden, and a community's angry response to violating taboos. "You were curious about black ... I was curious about white," Snipes says when the couple parts ways.

But in general, reviewers found the film uneven. "Despite some powerful scenes and performances, the film is sadly underwritten. The central relationship is neither adequately explained nor realistically depicted, with the film emitting much heat but little illumination on race relations, black self-hatred, or the allure of sex with the Other," said one. Critic Charles Taylor, examining the ways Hollywood has presented interracial relationships in a Salon.com article, "Black and White and Taboo All Over," maintained that Lee real agenda was separatism—blacks and whites staying apart. "Lee pays lip service to the way each character is rejected by family and friends as a result of the affair,"

Taylor wrote, "but he can't hide his disgust with the relationship . . . . Lee's message is a blatant version of the thought that hovers in [Katherine] Hepburn's and [Spencer] Tracy's minds in the [Stanley] Kramer film [*Guess Who's Coming to Dinner?*]: 'Wouldn't you be happier with your own kind?'"

As though answering "Yes," Lee's next film would be devoted to his hero, Malcolm X, a champion of separatism, black identity, and black self-determination.

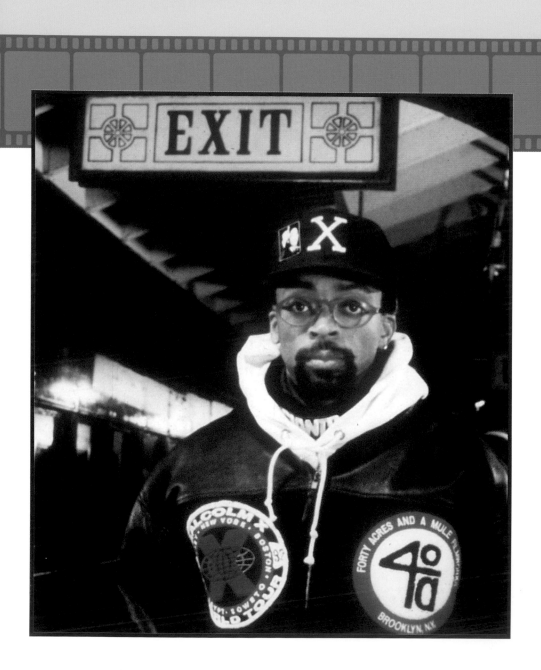

Perhaps Lee's most daunting task as a director was to bring the film biography of cultural activist Malcolm X to life. Getting the film off the ground forced Lee to confront some of the film industry's most powerful studios and producers.

Chapter 5

"Malcolm-Mania"

I've never really had any struggles with studios telling me what to do, I've been very fortunate. The one time when we really had a scrape was on Malcolm X *. . . That was one of the worst periods I had in my life.*

—Spike Lee

TO CAPTURE ON film the life of Malcolm X was not only an artistic challenge to Lee—it was a personal mission. He admired the legendary black leader deeply, and in deciding to make a biographical portrait of his hero, he committed himself to seeing through to the end the biggest project he had even undertaken. He would have to supervise months of research, explore dozens of key locations, and push for financing nearly three times' greater than the budget of his previous film, *Jungle Fever*. And there were plenty of immediate obstacles to be overcome.

To start with, for example, he had to seize the right and authority to make the picture.

Warner Brothers already had plans underway to make a biopic about Malcolm X, directed by Norman Jewison, whose 1988 film *Moonstruck* with Cher and Nicholas Cage had been a hit with audiences. Lee mounted a campaign to wrest away the film from Jewison, but retain Warner Brothers' backing. Using the press to publicize his cause, Lee said in an interview with the *New York Times,* that he had a "big problem" with a white director telling the life of Malcolm X.

Jewison, apparently unwilling to enter a public debate about race, bowed out. Spike got the nod from Warner Brothers.

Next, he asked for $33 million to make the film, arguing that a budget that size was needed to show the development of Malcolm X from street hustler to civil rights leader—not just the brief period when he came to the attention of whites. Warner Brothers agreed to $20 million for a two-hour and 15-minute film, pointing out that Lee's five previous films combined grossed less than $100 million in the United States. To show his faith in his vision, Lee countered by brokering deals to foreign rights to the film, worth an additional $8.5 million, and added part of his $3 million salary to the production budget.

But then, seemingly out of nowhere, an open letter appeared in *Ebony* magazine, submitted by a group calling itself the United Front to Preserve the Memory of Malcolm X and the Cultural Revolution, led by poet and activist Amiri

Baraka (formerly LeRoi Jones). "Our distress about Spike's making a film on Malcolm is based on our analysis of the [exploitative] films he has already made," the letter read in part. In short, they didn't think Spike was the man for the job.

"His whole criticism centered around the idea that I was bourgeois and all these other things, too middle class," Lee told *American Visions* magazine. "I had to be a card-carrying member of the Socialist Party. I just look at it like a lot of people had their own agendas, and I think with Baraka, a lot had to do with jealousy." In any case, the storm blew over.

The road to making *Malcolm X* got smoother in at least one place, however. The actor Lee wanted for the lead, Denzel Washington—also the lead in *Mo' Better Blues*—was eager to take the role. Washington had played Malcolm X in an off-Broadway play in 1981, *When the Chickens Come Home to Roost*. He had always wanted to do more with the part. When Lee approached him in 1991, he was more than ready to jump in again.

On the other hand, the screenplay Lee inherited was in tatters. Arnold Perl, who died in 1971, had finished an outline for a cinematic life of Malcolm X more than twenty years before. Over the years, a handful of other screen-writing heavyweights had taken a stab at fleshing it out, including James Baldwin, Calder Willingham, David Mamet, David Bradley, and Charles Fuller. The result was that the script's freshness was gone and the story failed to hang together. Lee read it, put it aside, and realized it would have to undergo yet another top-to-bottom rewrite.

Shooting began on September 16, 1991. As he had with several of his other films, Lee used bodyguards from the Nation of Islam to protect the sets and keep back onlookers, even though Nation of Islam Minister Louis Farrakhan was concerned about the film's portrayal of Elijah Muhammad's sacred legacy. "Minister Farrakhan's threats weren't even veiled," Lee said. "But, I think it would be too risky for them to try some [expletive] with me." The cast and crew filmed in New York City and Fishkill, New York; the Essex County Prison in Newark, NJ, built during or shortly after the Civil War; Boston, Massachusetts; Mecca, Saudi Arabia; Soweto, South Africa; and Egypt.

The story is told in three sections almost like acts in a play. The first begins with the troubled childhood of Malcolm Little, whose father is murdered by the Ku Klux Klan and whose mother is institutionalized for insanity. Malcolm grows up and gets a job as a Pullman porter, calling himself Detroit Red. During WWII, Little and his friend Shorty (Lee) are hustlers in Boston's Black Roxbury section.

Malcolm then joins a numbers gang in Harlem and ends up in Charleston State Prison. The second section follows his life in prison, where a fellow inmate, Baines (Albert Hall), introduces him to the teachings of the Nation of Islam and Elijah Muhammad (Al Freeman, Jr.). Malcolm Little adopts the name Malcolm X.

The third section follows Malcolm's religious conversion as a disciple of the Honorable Elijah Mohammed (Al Freeman Jr.). During his fervent immersion into the Nation of Islam, he becomes an incendiary speaker for the movement and marries Betty Shabazz (Angela Bassett), a Muslim nurse. Malcolm X preaches a doctrine of hate against the white man, but a pilgrimage to Mecca softens his beliefs. He tries to break free of the strict dogma of the Nation of Islam, but is finally assassinated, allegedly by members of the Nation.

But when the film wrapped, and Lee believed there was clearly three hours' worth of story to be told on the screen, Warner Brothers stepped in and pulled the plug on post-production financing.

A personal mission for Lee, *Malcolm X* featured stellar performances from Denzel Washington (as Malcolm) and Al Freeman, Jr. (as Elijah Mohammed). After Warner Brothers cut post-production funding, Lee raised funds himself, calling on entertainment industry leaders like Bill Cosby and Oprah Winfrey. Shortly thereafter, Warner Brothers restored funding to the film.

"I've never really had any struggles with studios telling me what to do, I've been very fortunate. The one time when we really had a scrape was on *Malcolm X*, where we had a big row with Warner Brothers who did not want the film at that length," Lee told the audience at the 1996 Imagination Conference in San Francisco. The film was already $5 million over budget and still unedited. To put the screws to Lee, Warner Brothers allowed the bond company underwriting the film to take direct control. His funds were about to be cut off. The choice was: Do it Warner Brothers' way and shorten the film, or else. His editing staff each received a FedEx letter telling them they had been fired. "That was one of the worst periods I had in my life," Lee said.

He responded the only way that seemed logical. Malcolm X was a great man to many black Americans. So, Spike got on the phone to wealthy black Americans in entertainment. "In doing my research on Malcolm, one of the things Malcolm talked about was self-reliance—African-Americans relying on each other and not expecting other people to bail them out," Lee told the San Francisco audience. "So taking a lesson from Malcolm, I made a list of prominent African-Americans who had some bank."

At the top of his list was Bill Cosby. Nervously, Lee phoned him, made some small talk, and then asked how his wife was. Cosby responded, "Spike, how much do you need?" Lee cautiously asked for a "low number." Cosby said he tell his accountant to make out a check. "I took the subway into Manhattan, got the check, and ran to the bank and deposited it," Lee said. Then he continued working his way down his list of phone numbers:

> The next call was to Ms. Winfrey. Again, we exchanged a few pleasantries, I asked her how Desmond was, and I said you been really looking slender the last couple of days, and I told her the predicament we were in, and she said, 'How much do you need, Spike?' And I told her. It worked with Bill, so I decided 'let me take a chance', and I gave her a high number— and she wrote the check. Then I called Magic Johnson, and Magic came through. Then I called my main man, Michael Jordan, and knowing that Michael was very competitive I told him what Magic gave. Then Tracy Chapman, and then the-artist-formally-known-as-Prince, and Janet Jackson, all these people came through and wrote six-figure checks.

Warner Brothers was publicly embarrassed. "Warner Brothers understood exactly what it was to have these people writing checks for me to continue," Lee told *American Visions.* "Two days later, they started funding us. That is power." But he also pointed out that Hollywood is a highly competitive place "and the playing field is not level [for blacks]. So if you're an African-American, you know that you have more hurdles thrown in your way, more obstacles. And you can bitch and moan about it, or you can try to jump those hurdles and smash those obstacles. And it's not fair, and that's the way it is."

One of most important challenges of filming *Malcolm X* was recreating the look of Harlem during the 1940s and 50s. Set designers took over a section of 3rd Avenue between 118th and 121st streets in New York City and went to work. Restoration specialists brought back to life Herbert's Diamonds, the African Bookstore, and the Apollo Theater, all of which appear prominently in photographs of Malcolm X speaking to crowds. To recreate Temple Number 7 and the Moslem luncheonette located below it, crews took over a building on 116th street, gutted it, then put in floors, ceilings, and walls. Lee wanted to use the actual Audubon Ballroom where Malcolm X was assassinated, but rain had come in through the roof and the floors had buckled. Total estimated cost of repairs: $750,000—more than the budget of *She's Gotta Have It.* Instead, construction moved to a large room at the Hotel Diplomat on 43rd street. In 4-5 days' time, the room had been repainted and a stage erected to film the scene of Malcolm X's assassination. In all, there were over 100 locations used during six months of filming.

When *Malcolm X* was released in 1992, Barry Reardon, Warner Brothers' president of distribution, conceded, "Spike did a fabulous job. He knows theaters, he's very smart. This is Oscars all the way."

In the meantime, well before its release, the movie had achieved a tremendous stature in the minds of moviegoers, and its impact on culture was already obvious. So much so, in fact, that Lee was accused of cashing-in on the name of his hero. A bold "X," appeared on baseball caps, posters, postcards, and T-shirts. A plastic Malcolm X doll appeared in grocery stores, complete with podium and audiocassette. The *New Yorker* satirized the outpouring of promotional merchandise—all of it marketed by Lee himself through Spike's Joint, a chain of stores—with a cartoon that showed a hotel doorman, a man walking a dog on a leash, and the dog, all wearing black Malcolm X caps.

Lee defended himself against charges that he had exploited an American legend. "I've always felt that if opportunities came to me, I should take advantage of them," he told *American Visions*. "I was not going to limit myself by saying that I would not do anything outside the movies."

By the time moviegoers crowded into theaters to see *Malcolm X*, the build-up to its release may have raised expectations too high. The movie opens with a pair of disturbing, in-your-face images: the notorious video footage of unarmed black motorist Rodney King being beaten by white Los Angeles policemen, and an American flag burning down into the shape of an "X." From there however, perhaps because the film has to pace itself over three and a half hours, *Malcolm X* quietly runs out of steam. Although it has all of the hallmarks of "A Spike Lee Joint"—flashy costumes, dance numbers, hoodlums, and inventive camera angles—the film is a rather traditional biography. Malcolm X's gangster years are cleaned-up and his politics are toned down. In general, reviewers criticized the film's length and its mildness. Despite black historian

While his films had long been criticized as too confrontational, Lee's *Malcolm X* drew the reverse commentary—with critics charging that the film ran out of steam and diluted Malcolm's political views.

Cornel West's observation that "Malcolm X articulated Black rage in a manner unprecedented in American History," *Malcolm X* the movie presented a man who seemed to want to build bridges to white America instead of burning them.

After a disappointingly short run at the box office, *Malcolm X* took up its place on the shelves of video stores.

Wrote one online reviewer, "The Hollywood blockbuster has never been a congenial medium for overtly political filmmaking but, in the final analysis, *Malcolm X* must be viewed as the triumph of Spike Lee's will."

After *Malcolm X*, Lee sought a major departure from the films he had made. In *Crooklyn*, he returns to his Brooklyn roots. Co-written by Spike, his sister Joie, and brother Cinque, the delivers a touching and often funny portrait of black family life.

Chapter 6

Trial and Error

. . . for me, being a filmmaker includes making documentary films, short films, music videos, commercials, and feature narrative films.

—Spike Lee

MALCOLM X HAD been Lee's trial by fire—a test to see whether he could juggle the demands of a big-budget feature whose total running time, when completed, was twice as long as many full-length films. By comparison, other film-making projects didn't seem as demanding. The next ten years saw Spike writing, directing, and releasing a flurry of productions ranging from movies, commercials, and made-for-TV documentaries, to live performances turned into films.

In mid-1993, Lee began shooting his seventh feature film, the comedy *Crooklyn*, a major departure in story and treatment from his earlier films. A largely autobiographical look back at a jazz musician, his wife, and their children in Brooklyn of the 1970s, *Crooklyn* was an attempt to "expand the subject matter of the films we do," Lee said. He said he wanted to get away from "hip-hop, drug, gangsta rap, urban, inner-city" movies. His aim was to make a movie to which black families could take their children.

Co-scripted by Joie Susannah Lee, Cinque Lee, and Spike—their first collaboration together—the film seeks to look at the world through a child's eyes, in this case the coming-of-age of a young black girl. Shot on location in Brooklyn, the film opens with the kind of cultural montage that Spike relishes: kids wearing Afros, 1970s television, and the sounds of soul music wafting into scenes. As the only girl in a family full of boys, nine-year-old Troy Carmichael (Zelda Harris) has to be strong, smart and quick with her fists if necessary. Her mother (Alfre Woodard) is portrayed as an angry, overwrought woman who keeps her family going on a teachers' salary and food stamps, while her husband (Delroy Lindo) hangs onto dreams of making it big in jazz.

As in *She's Gotta Have It* and *Do the Right Thing*, Lee accurately renders the noisy, intimate feeling of an urban neighborhood. Over the course of a summer, Troy fights with her brothers, learns to steal from a grocery store, rebels against her mother, suffers her parents' arguments, and takes a wild visit to see a cousin in Virginia. As happened in the real Lee family, the mother dies suddenly of cancer, and the family is left grief-stricken, but doggedly intact. (During filming, Spike took a break to marry Linette Lewis, a lawyer he had been dating for over a year.)

Crooklyn was released in 1994 to lukewarm reviews. Many critics said Lee was at his best getting audiences riled up. Instead, *Crooklyn* had the feel of a home movie about an affectionate family and a summer they would never forget.

Then, as though immersing himself in the kind of stronger subject he feels most comfortable with, in 1995 Lee co-wrote and directed *Clockers*.

At first, Lee was reluctant to take on the project. The subject of Richard Price's 1991 novel *Clockers* is drug-dealing. "I didn't say yes right away because I didn't want to make another gangster, shoot 'em up, hip-hop drug film," Lee told Britain's *The Guardian* newspaper. "I felt that genre was really limping into its last gasp." Director Martin Scorsese and actor Robert De Niro were set to make the film, but then Lee saw an opportunity. He could shift the story's emphasis away from the white police officer hero, and focus on the African-American victims of crime and violence. Scorsese and De Niro bowed out of the project after Lee persuaded Warner Brothers to buy the rights to the film for him. Then he set to work transforming it into a "A Spike Lee Joint."

Rewritten, *Clockers* tells the story of two brothers—one a drug dealer, the other a straight-laced family man—who become suspects in a mysterious murder investigation in the black community. Lee cast first-time actor Mekhi Phifer as the tormented young drug dealer, and changed the locale from Jersey City to Brooklyn. "We took a different approach with that film, so it was really the deglorification of violence and this whole hip-hop infatuation with drugs and guns and killing people. That's why we had that opening credit sequence where you see crime-scene photos of bullet-ridden bodies from drugs stuff," Lee explained to *The Guardian*.

Some reviewers objected to the major changes Lee had made to the story in Price's novel, but *Time* magazine critic Richard Schickel praised Lee's ambition, saying the film is "is more than a murder mystery and more than a study in character conflict. At its best, it is an intense and complex portrait of an urban landscape on which the movies' gaze has not often fallen."

In 1996, Lee released two films, *Girl 6* and *Get On the Bus*. The first was the story of a frustrated young actress who gleefully takes a job as a phone-sex worker. Critics panned it and loud objections were raised to Lee's portrayal of women, a problem that had been leveled at his films on and off since *She's Gotta Have It*. His second film released that year, however, *Get on the Bus* —financed by 15 African-American men, including Johnnie Cochran, Will Smith, and Wesley Snipes— marked a turning point in Lee's career.

His inspiration for the film came from the Million Man March, an event the year before organized by Louis Farrakhan, the leader of the Nation of Islam. Scripted by TV writer Reggie Rock Bythewood, *Get On the Bus* assembles a cross-section of African-American men and follows them on their trip to the march in Washington, D.C.

The result is an interesting blend of comedy and

Inspired by the Million Man March on Washington in 1995, *Get On the Bus* follows a diverse group of African-American men on their journey to the nation's capital. Lee used his characters—from a reformed gangbanger to a Republican businessman—to voice a range of perspectives.

drama. In a sense, it's an old-fashioned movie where the power of the performances by talented actors is the pleasure of the film, not watching a political message uncoil from Lee's hand. The passengers run the gamut: an old failure, a young upstart actor, a gentle cop, a reformed gangbanger, a homosexual couple, a silent Muslim, a Republican businessman, an estranged father reunited with his gangbanger son and chained to him by court order, a truck driver, an aspiring filmmaker/witness ("Spike Lee Jr.," as one of the characters calls him), and the bus driver/spokesperson.

"[W]e wanted everybody to have their say on this bus, because in a lot of ways each person has to stand for some ideology or some aspect of African-American men," Lee told *IndieNetwork.com.*

One of the biggest challenges from a technical standpoint was capturing performances inside an actual bus on the road. Spike elected to using the kind of cameras he was schooled on during his graduate student days at NYU's Tisch School of the Arts:

> It was very difficult. A large part of the film was actually shot on that bus while it was moving. The small area was one of the reasons we elected to shoot with Super 16. I like to shoot two cameras at a time, but with two 35mm cameras in that space we would have been straining our necks. Super 16 gave us a lot more flexibility. . . . A lot of this film was shot hand-held, so when you add it up, it makes sense to go Super 16. The cameras were lighter.

Get On the Bus' realism and touching performances earned praised from reviewers who congratulated Lee for putting more emphasis on dialogue and character development than action, sound, and striking visuals— the tripod supporting most of his earlier films.

The following year, Lee returned to his interest in illuminating black history with a documentary for HBO cable television—*4 Little Girls*, the story of a bombing in

Birmingham, Alabama in September 1963 that killed three African-American girls at the height of the civil rights movement. Lee was concerned that "a lot of young people, both black and white, that really don't know about the civil rights struggle and civil rights movement, and African-Americans in particular who today are bearing the fruits of everybody who had to sacrifice and struggle," he told the online magazine *indieWIRE*. He was convinced there was a need to revisit this particularly painful incident in history. An especially difficult moment occurred when Lee was doing research and came upon the morgue photographs of the dead children.

"When the clerk called the photos out, we were startled and taken aback," he told indieWIRE. "You can imagine what 20 sticks of dynamite can do. But when you see the results, it literally brings tears to your eyes. I have to be honest with you, I was not 100 percent sure whether I should include those shots. The postmortem photographs. But I decided if we didn't linger on them, it would be tasteful. They reinforce the horror and the crime that was committed . . . "

4 Little Girls received an Emmy and an Oscar nomination. Said *Time* magazine, "Lee's eloquent film does justice to the young martyrs and to those who guaranteed that the girl's deaths, while tragic, would not also be meaningless."

Over the years, however, Lee had not written an original screenplay—not since *Jungle Fever*. So when his wife suggested he try his hand at another, he agreed. "I wanted to do something about fathers and sons and also forgiveness," Lee told *The Guardian*. "Can a son forgive his father who is directly responsible for killing his mother?"

The result was *He Got Game* (the expression means

"he can play"), released in 1998. The story portrays the troubled relationship between a high school basketball star and his long-absent father, played by Denzel Washington. Writing in the *New York Times*, long-time film critic Janet Maslin, said, "Mr. Lee now returns full blast to what he does best. Basketball, bold urban landscapes, larger-than-life characters, and red-hot visual pyrotechnics are the strong points of Mr. Lee's three-ring circus, not to mention the central presence of Denzel Washington."

Unfortunately, the story tended to strain audience's credulity. Jake Shuttlesworth (Washington) is a prisoner serving a long sentence in Attica. When the film opens, he is called off the outdoor basketball court to see the warden. It seems that Jake's son, Jesus (Ray Allen), is the leading high-school basketball prospect in the country, and one of the colleges he is considering attending is the governor's alma mater. A fanatical hoops fan, the governor desperately wants Jesus to go to enroll there, and, through the warden, offers Jake a deal: If he can convince his son to sign a letter of intent the governor will substantially shorten Jake's sentence. Jake is secretly released and sent to a sleazy hotel in Brooklyn's Coney Island accompanied by two guards who have orders to kill him if he tries to escape. He has one week to perform his mission.

"If this sounds impossibly corny, it is," commented a reviewer in Salon.com, "but Lee pulls it off surprisingly well. And Lee the sentimentalist is vastly preferable to Lee the didact," meaning that part of the film's appeal was that it lacked Lee's usual preachiness. At the box office, the film did less than average business.

The following year, Lee revisited a brief era in his

Again calling on the talents of actor Denzel Washington, Lee's *He Got Game* examines the relationship between a high school basketball star and his long-absent father.

youth—the summer of 1977 when serial killer David Berkowitz terrorized the Bronx neighborhood of New York City. That had been the summer Lee had embarked on being a filmmaker for the first time, touring the streets with a Super 8-mm camera and recording the sights and sounds. "I was 20 years old in New York at the time . . . I remember the heat, the World Series, the disco," he told *Filmcritic.com.*

But mainly because of the film's title, *Summer of Sam*, Lee was forced to handle a barrage of protests from the families of Berkowtiz's victims, and even—most surprising of all—complaints from the convicted killer himself. Berkowitz attacked Lee for "this madness, the ugliness of the past resurfacing again—all because some people want to make some money," according to an article in *Salon.com.* In a Sunday *New York Times* article, victims' relatives accused Lee of insensitivity, claiming that the movie, based on the events of the case as they unfolded in the summer of 1977, would reopen painful wounds. Lee responded that he was not making a movie about the killer per se, but about the cloud of evil that hung over the city that year.

Nevertheless, following a pre-release screening of *Summer of Sam,* for Walt Disney studio executives, it was decided that the film's graphic violence and nudity went over the top. Disney demanded that certain scenes be dropped. Joe Roth, Disney studios chairman told Britain's BBC news, "He's still got work to do. He's got stuff in there that is rougher than I would like and I'm hoping at some point he will trim it out."

Even "trimmed out," the movie, when released in 1999, met with mixed reviews. Though the screenplay was well-acted, the topic continued to repel most moviegoers. Criticism about the film's frantic pace and Lee's treatment of Italian-Americas, women, and gays drew attention away from the film's merits. "In the end," said a reviewer for the online magazine *Flak*, "the film falls prey to Lee's cardboard stereotypes and his manic and constant need to have everything spiral wildly out of control."

Then came *Bamboozled* in 2000, "a 21st century minstrel show," as Spike called it, after which he stayed squarely behind the camera for his next two projects: filming live performances not created by his company, 40 Acres and Mule.

The Original Kings of Comedy started out as a cross-country concert tour of four black comics playing to packed houses starting in 1997. Ticket sales exceeded $50 million, making it the most attended comedy tour ever. Steve Harvey, D.L. Hughley, Cedric the Entertainer and Bernie Mac take the stage in ties and jackets to unleash a non-stop barrage of racy jokes and parodies of people's behavior. Filmed over two nights (February 26 & 27, 2000) in the Charlotte, North Carolina Coliseum, *The Original Kings of Comedy* is a relatively straightforward presentation of a concert. Lee remains focused on the stage show, allowing the comic momentum to ebb and flow naturally. By using digital video and sound, uncomplicated camerawork, and basic editing techniques, Lee draws the viewer in, creating a feeling of "you are there" as if in a seat at the concert. His aim is to document the event, not to interpret it.

Lee's success at filming a stage show and his interest in black history and culture intersected with *A Huey P. Newton Story* in 2001. Adapted from Roger Guenveur

The Original Kings of Comedy follows four African American comics during a two-night stop on their nationwide tour. Featuring Steve Harvey, D.L. Hughley, Cedric the Entertainer, and Bernie Mac, Kings was filmed unobtrusively by Lee, allowing viewers to feel they have a front row seat at the show.

Smith's Obie Award winning off-Broadway solo performance of the same name, the performance of *A Huey P. Newton Story* was shot before a live audience. Guenveur Smith speaks, unscripted, in Newton's own words. Lee added classic soul music, original compositions, and archival footage to put the historical leader of the Black Panthers into the context of his times. The production of *Huey* brought together Spike Lee, Huey Newton's heirs, PBS, the National Black Programming Consortium, KQED Public Television, the Ford Foundation and the African Heritage Network, among others, into a first-time ever creative and business partnership.

Whether as director, social critic, or both, Spike Lee has courted controversy at almost every turn. His unflinching commitment to confronting racism has earned him both critics and admirers worldwide.

Chapter 7

Spike vs. Everybody

As the most prominent black director in the American movie industry, he probably feels as if he were sprinting downcourt with no one to pass to and about five hundred towering white guys between him and the basket.

—Terrence Rafferty
film critic, *New Yorker* magazine

AS THE MOST important African-American filmmaker of his generation, Spike Lee is under a lot of pressure. On the one hand, he wants to make films that speak to experiences of black

Americans—their history, hopes and culture. Most of his films are, at some level, about black identity. On the other hand, mainstream movie-going audiences tend not to be drawn to those subjects, leaving him with a tough choice. To paraphrase Shakespeare's *Hamlet,* it's "To be Spike, or not to be Spike—that is the question."

To begin with, Lee has built his career on the belief that black audiences are hungry for black films— movies made by black writers, directors, and actors for black filmgoers. From a historical perspective, he's right. For as long as movies have been shown inside darkened rooms—for more than a century now—blacks have almost always been presented in demeaning roles that encouraged racism. There was a breakthrough of sorts in the 1970s. Several films featuring African- American actors in stories involving drugs and violence did well at the box office. What followed was a rash of "blaxploitation" shoot-'em-ups, usually set in urban ghettoes. Hollywood eagerly served up gun-toting black anti-heroes, but that created yet another stereo- type, and still not a very flattering one. Until the arrival of black directors like Spike Lee and John Singleton, the relationship between Hollywood and blacks has been shallow and lopsided.

To find his own voice as a screenwriter and director— one who can present blacks authentically—Lee has looked to his own life. This typical of the best directors and screenwriters: to find the meaning in his own experiences and turn them, though artistic skill, in films that strike a chord with audiences.

He did this in two of his films that critics have since called his finest: *She's Gotta Have It* and *Do the Right Thing.* In the first, the sexual relationship between men and women was comically explored by asking a bold question: What if a black woman had the sexual appetite of most black men? As Nola Darling juggles three lovers at the same time, never feeling an ounce of concern, audiences are led amused, startled, and made uncomfortable all at the same time. In *Do the Right Thing*, violence is shown as a collision between who oppressed people and their antagonists, both of whom have lost the ability to understand, or even tolerate, each other any longer. It's a dilemma that occurs everywhere differences separate people.

But since those films, critics tend to agree that Lee seems to have accepted that separatism not only exists, but that it's also natural. Maybe, Lee seems to be saying, blacks and whites, men and women, gays and straights are separated by differences that can never be overcome. It's a pessimistic and anti-intellectual view, and one that has deprived him of more success at the box office.

One problem that crops up immediately with a separatist viewpoint in a movie is that crossover audiences aren't interested. Most of Lee's films are heavy with black English, for example, ignoring the fact that most white people have trouble understanding it. So in a mixed audience, black viewers will laugh while whites feel left out. In addition, Lee enjoys making jokes at white's expense—a reversal of the times when blacks were the butt of jokes in films. But again, the effect tends to chill the enthusiasm of white audiences and reviewers.

Separatism also depends on seeing other people as types: loud-mouthed, abusive Italians; insensitive whites; brutal cops; two-timing women; corrupt officials—and the list goes on. Lee depends on cutout characters as a way of making his conflicts clear, but it has brought him a great deal of criticism. In a review of *He Got Game*, for instance, Salon.com film reviewer Gary Kamiya complained:

> [Lee's] muddled racial litany is depressingly familiar: He takes a stacked-deck plot in which racist, hypocritical, wimpy or otherwise lame white people befoul the lives of the black protagonists, throws in some equally lame black characters and one or two decent but peripheral white ones, punches things up with one or two audacious set-pieces of cinematic bang-bang, and ties the whole ungainly thing together with mawkishly sentimental music. The hip, loose, comedic elements in his work clash incongruously with its dogmatism [preachiness].

Some groups—feminists and gays, in particular—have lost patience with what they allege is Lee's unfair presentation of them as types, a claim he angrily disputes. The following exchange took place between Lee and an interviewer for *The Advocate*, a national gay and lesbian online newsmagazine:

> Q: *In* Clockers *the kids who are working the street, the clockers, call the homicide detectives "homo-cide." Does your use of the words* homo *and* faggot *in your films contribute to homophobia?*

> A: No. What gets me is, have you ever called up Martin Scorsese and asked him how many times he uses the [expletive] word *nigger?* In *Mean Streets,* in *Good Fellas,* in *Raging Bull?* This is the way these characters speak. Because I use the words *faggot* and *homo,* people try to pin me as [expletive] homophobic, and that's [expletive]. If homosexuals don't think people call them "faggots" and "homos," then they're stupid.

In *Clockers*, Lee tackles the world of street drugs, cops, and the daily challenges faced by urban black communities. His insistence that his characters use realistic street language has inspired disputes with the gay and lesbian press.

Q: *Well—*

A: Wait a [expletive] minute. Has anybody ever gone to Quentin Tarantino and asked him how many times he uses the [expletive] word *nigger* in *True Romance, Reservoir Dogs,* and *Pulp Fiction*? He uses the word, and nobody says a [expletive] thing about it.

Q: *I understand that—*

A: You don't understand, because I'm always getting this [expletive] from the homosexual community—that I'm homophobic. Because I have a character in a movie say "faggot," that means that automatically Spike Lee is homophobic, and I'm sick of this [expletive][expletive]. Why are gays always able to make that distinction with Martin Scorsese—and they don't make it with me?

Q: *When the same respect black people have struggled for is not extended to our community, it takes us by surprise. You can see that, right?*

A: Yeah, I could see that taking you by surprise. I can see that, sure.

Q: *So I think that's one of the reasons why you're singled out and not Scorsese.*

A: You're saying, Scorsese's white, so he doesn't know better? But, Spike, you're black, so you should know better? I'm not buying that. I know everybody looks after their own, but you just can't talk about being antigay and then dismiss racism.

Q: *In your second film,* School Daze, *a rival fraternity ridicules the Gamma Phi Gammas by calling them fags.*

A: That movie is about my four years at Morehouse College. When I went to school, for good or worse, homosexuals were ridiculed. Morehouse has always had a large gay presence, it being a predominantly black-male school. Because of that, I think homophobia is probably bigger there than at a coed school. By showing it I don't think I'm endorsing it. It's a reality. The gay community should know African-Americans are more homophobic than anybody.

Q: *Why do you say that?*

A: For the most part we're very conservative, and we still have a very strong religious background. Because we still have a strong sense of the black church, homosexuality is frowned upon. That's just my sense.

Lee's outspokenness and enjoyment of controversy tends to further alienate audiences and drive the wedge deeper between himself and mainstream America. In 1999, a month after the Columbine High School shootings, Lee was asked by a reporter at the Cannes Film Festival what he thought might help end gun violence. Referring to National Rifle Association President Charlton Heston, Lee suggested, "Shoot him—with a .44-caliber Bulldog." At the time, Lee had a contract with the U.S. Navy to film six Navy commercials. Leading members of Congress demanded that the Navy drop Lee because of his remark. Spike later said he meant it as a joke.

He again made headlines when he called the Mel Gibson's 2000 film *The Patriot* "a disgrace" and "Hollywood propaganda" because of its once-over-lightly treatment of slavery in the story. "When talking about the history of this great country, one can never forget, leave out or whatever, that America was built upon the genocide of Native Americans and the enslavement of African people. To say otherwise is criminal," Lee wrote in the *Hollywood Reporter*'s weekly guest column. Later that year, he slammed Will Smith for appearing as a mystical and spiritual golf caddy in *The Legend of Bagger Vance*, criticizing him for helping paint a pleasant picture of the South during the 1930s.

Lee is quick to point out films where he sees "Hollywood propaganda." He criticized both *The Patriot* and *The Legend of Bagger Vance* as ignoring critical racial issues of the 1770s and 1930s.

"When Lee writes and speaks to the media, he is much more political and acerbic than his movies are," Alan Stone wrote for the *Boston Review*, in an analysis of Lee's work. "Many people who know him only from the pages of *The New York Times* have decided that he is a vicious and dangerous. . . ."

It's unfortunate that the man and his anger has come to obscure his work. Lee has blazed the way for countless black actors, writers, and directors—vaulting over the wall that kept them out of Hollywood, except as bit-players in movies. "Spike put this trend in vogue," Warner Bros. executive vice-president Mark Canton told *Time*. "His talent opened the door for others."

But Lee makes no apologies for his stances, either in public or on the screen.

The *Sydney* (Australia) *Morning Herald* asked Lee, "A lot of people call you the angriest black man in America. Is that true?"

"The press thinks I am," Lee replied. "I don't walk around in a perpetual state of anger 24/7. Nonetheless, I still think there's a lot of things for us to be angry about. There's a lot of African-American athletes and entertainers who would speak out about what they know in their heart is wrong, but don't because it might have some adverse effect on their paycheck. You know, mum is the word. I'm not one of them."

Although outspoken, Lee has never claimed to be a spokesperson for African-Americans in general, but rather to point out the hypocrisies and inconsistencies where he sees them.

Chapter 8

Spike on Spike

I guess you could call me an instigator.

—Spike Lee

ALTHOUGH OUTSPOKEN, SPIKE LEE does not see himself as a spokesperson.

"I have never, ever felt that I was a spokesperson for Afro-Americans in this country," he told the online magazine *indieWIRE*. "I understand that the media is trying to pinpoint individuals that they do think speak for the masses or particular groups." There was a time, Lee said, when the media sought him out to comment on issues and events affecting black people. But Spike learned not to take the bait every time. "Now I guess I really consciously pick and choose sponsoring an issue that I want to talk about."

Nevertheless, he realizes that he is thought of, in most people minds, as a black director and that status implies that he has certain values.

"I have no problems with white America looking at me as a black man because I understand the mind-set and where we are in this country," he said in the *indieWIRE* interview. "I think the majority of white Americans are unable to look at somebody black and not the skin of their color first. That's just the reality."

"I do not get upset if journalists want to put 'black' in front of the word 'film-maker,'" he explained to *The Guardian* newspaper. "I know there are other people like Whoopi Goldberg who feel much different about that and get mad, but I'm not gonna get any ulcers or lose any hair over that."

White journalists, he said, expose their prejudices by the attitude they take toward his work. "I can tell exactly how white journalists feel about black people by the questions they ask," he told the *New York Times* during a promotion of *Do the Right Thing*. "'Hey, Spike,' they'll say, 'this Bedford-Stuyvesant looks too clean. Hey, Spike, there's no garbage on the street. Hey, Spike, where are the drugs? Where's the muggers? Hey, I don't see any teen-age women throwing their babies out of windows.' Those were these people's perception of black people in general." He said he prefers to set most of his films in New York City because that's where he lives— in the neighborhood where he grew up, in fact—and that's where he's the most comfortable.

His goal as a filmmaker, he says, was never to portray more positive images of black Americans, but to present ones that are more realistic. He said that if he only focused on positive images, "It would be like a straight-jacket," he told an audience during a panel presentation at Harvard University. "It is not dramatic and it is not realistic." This brings him into conflict with blacks at times. In an interview carried by *American Visions* magazine, Lee stated, "It is a fallacy that all my critics are white."

The way he keeps his balance artistically is by remaining an independent filmmaker, explaining to *Premier* magazine that it is "the best of both worlds . . . I don't have to scrape around for money. I go . . . to Hollywood for my financing. It doesn't really mess with my creativity, because I have the final cut and the control over the film that I would have had if I'd raised the money all by myself."

The key to blacks gaining more influence in Hollywood and popular media in general, he said, is becoming a "gatekeeper," as he terms it. "There is not one African-American executive in Hollywood that can green-light a picture," he pointed out in an interview with Salon.com. "I'm not talking about Wesley [Snipes] or Will [Smith] or Denzel [Washington] or Chris Tucker or Chris Rock. I'm talking about suits. These are the people who are called the 'gatekeepers.' I think we have to gain access to those positions."

In addition, Lee believes that too much mystery surrounds the craft of filmmaking. It's one that can be learned, and now with the availability of digital video, young up-and-coming filmmakers can practice their art for a fraction of what it once cost to make a movie—even a student film. Like many of his fellow directors, Lee is coming around to preferring digital video for many of his projects. For *Bamboozled*, Lee and his cinematographer Ellen Kuras didn't like the look of Beta, DigiBeta or high definition digital, and went with miniDV instead, using a battery of Sony VX1000 cameras. "With this film it makes sense because it was about a television show," Lee says. "And we also had a 132-page script and not a lot of days. . . . We were able to shoot eight, nine, 10 cameras at a time. And it enabled us to put in the run-and-gun offense. So we were able to just shoot."

Branford Marsalis remembers that Lee's directing style is equally to the point: "The most that Spike ever tells an actor is, 'Here's the script. Ready? Action!' And it used to be very funny for me to watch the seasoned veterans say, 'Well Spike, what is your vision?' Spike says, 'I paid you good money to act. That's my vision. Now act. Action!'"

To young filmmakers, he offers two pieces of advice: get experience and make connections.

"I don't want to make a blanket statement, but when you're a young filmmaker I think an agent can only help you once you've established yourself," he explained to *IndieNetwork.com*. "If you haven't directed a feature film yet, you basically have to do it yourself. Or try to align yourself with other people who are going in the same direction you're going." In his own life, his biggest influences have been sports figures, not filmmakers surprisingly: Mohammed Ali, Michael Jordan, Willie Mays. Interestingly, he believes musicians are the greatest artists, not filmmakers.

In the near term, Lee told *The Guardian* newspaper, his goals are basic: "Try to become a better filmmaker, become a better storyteller. I think filmmakers are storytellers.

Between film projects, Lee still finds time to relax—as does here with his family at the 1999 Women's NBA All Star game.

But I'm very happy that I still make films and I still get immense pleasure from them, and that's what makes me happy. I say that knowing that I'm very fortunate because very few people get to do what they love, and I think most people go to their grave having slaved over a job they didn't enjoy. So I say my prayers every night."

Asked whether he would encourage his daughter Satchel to go into filmmaking, Spike told *IndieNetwork.com*, "Yes. I would want her to be behind the camera, not in front of the camera. That's where the power is."

1957 March 20, Shelton "Spike" Lee born in Atlanta, Georgia

1975 Graduates John Dewey High School in New York City; enters Morehouse College, Atlanta, Georgia

1977 Mother dies of breast cancer; spends the summer going around New York City filming street life

1979 Graduates from Morehouse College with a BA in Mass Communications

1980 Enters New York University's Institute of Film and Televsion, Tisch School of the Arts in the three-year film program

1982 Wins the 1982 Student Academy award for his film, *Joe's Bed-Stuy Barbershop: We Cut Heads*

1983 Graduates with a Masters of Fine Arts from NYU

1986 Wins the Los Angeles Film Critics New Generation award and the Prix de Jeunesse at the Cannes Film Festival for *She's Gotta Have It*

1992 Joins Board of Trustees at Morehouse College; teaches as a visiting professor at Harvard University

1993 Marries Tonya Linette Lewis, an attorney

1994 Daughter Satchel Lewis born

1997 Son Jackson Lewis born

1986 *She's Gotta Have It*

1988 *School Daze*

1989 *Do the Right Thing*

1990 *Mo' Better Blues*

1991 *Jungle Fever*

1992 *Malcolm X*

1994 *Crooklyn*

1995 *Clockers*
Lumière et Compagnie

1996 *Girl 6*
Get on the Bus

1997 *4 Little Girls*

1998 *He Got Game*
Freak (TV)

1999 *Summer of Sam*

2000 *Original Kings of Comedy, The*
Bamboozled

2001 *A Huey Newton Story* (TV)

Executive Producer

1994 *Drop Squad*

1995 *New Jersey Drive*
Tales From The Hood

Student Films

1977 *Last Hustle in Brooklyn*

1980 *Answer, The*

1981 *Sarah*

1983 *Joe's Bed-Stuy Barbershop: We Cut Heads*

Short Films

1986 Saturday Night Live: *Horn of Plenty*

1989 MTV: *Five One Minute Spots*

1991 HBO: *Iron Mike Tyson*

1995 HBO: *Real Sports "John Thompson" Coach*

Books

1988 *Spike Lee's Gotta Have It: Inside Guerrilla Filmmaking*

1989 *Uplift the Race: The Construction Of* School Daze

1990 *Do The Right Thing: A Spike Lee Joint*

1991 *Mo' Better Blues*

1992 *5 For 5*

1993 *By Any Means Necessary: The Trials and Tribulations of Making* Malcolm X

Lee entered New York University's Institute of Film and Television, where he won the 1982 Student Academy award for his film, *Joe's Bed-Stuy Barbershop: We Cut Heads*. He went on to win the Los Angeles Film Critics New Generation award and the Prix de Jeunesse at the Cannes Film Festival for his 1986 hit film *She's Gotta Have It*. He has been on the board of Morehouse College since 1992. He taught at Harvard as a visiting professor in 1992.

A Conversation with Spike Lee: Maverick Storyteller. Cinequest. 2001.
   [www.cinequest.org/2001/guide/spirit-lee.html]

A Huey P. Newton Story. Luna Rays Films. 2001.
   [http://starzsuperpak.com/se/betmovies/hp_newton/html/bios/spike.htm]

African American Filmmakers, African American Films: A Bibliography
   of Materials in the UC Berkeley Library. (Spike Lee).
   [www.lib.berkeley.edu/MRC/africanambib2.html#lee]

Akomfrah, John. Spike Lee (interview). *The Guardian.* November 18, 1999.
   [http://film.guardian.co.uk/Guardian_NFT/inter-view/0,4479,110609,00.html]

Altman, Susan. Spike Lee: Filmmaker/Actor. *Facts on File.* 1997.
   [http://www.pbs.org/immaw/Leebio.htm]

Bamboozled. New Line Productions (news release). 2001.
   [www.bamboozledmovie.com/film/filmmakers.html]

Bambury, Brent. Interview with Spike Lee. *Flick.* October 19, 2000.
   [www.lifenetwork.ca/flick/past/ep44/spike7.htm]

Baxter, Billy. The Spike Lee Interview. *Filmcritic.com.* No date.
   [http://efilmcritic.com/hbs.cgi?feature=141]

Bernotas, Bob. An Interview with Slide Hampton. *Online Trombone Journal.* 1994.
   [www.trombone.org/articles/library/slidehampton-int.asp]

Clark, Michael. Spike Lee: the Well Rounded Interview. *Well Rounded
   Entertainment.* October, 2000.
   [www.well-rounded.com/movies/reviews/spike_intv.html]

Cockburn, Alexander. Consuela's Return. *Maple Shade Records*
   (reprinted from *New York Press*). No date.
   [www.mapleshaderecords.com/artists/newyorkpress.html]

Daniloff, Miranda. Bamboozled with Spike Lee. Kennedy School of
   Government, Harvard University. November 6, 2000.
   [www.ksg.harvard.edu/news/spike_lee.htm]

Dirks, Tim. *The Birth of a Nation.* Greatest Films. 2002.
   [www.filmsite.org/birt.html]

Disney Tells Spike Lee to Cool It. BBC News. April 5, 1999.
   [http://news.bbc.co.uk/hi/english/entertainment/newsid_312000/312032.stm]

Do the Right Thing: A Brief Guide to Spike Lee. *HotWired.* 2001.
   [http://hotwired.lycos.com/popfeatures/96/23/lee.guide.html]

Elder, Larry. *The Ten Things You Can't Say in America* (first chapter).
   Bookradio.com. No date.
   [www.bookradio.com/books/031226660X/html/firstchapter.html]

Ellis, Joan. *Crooklyn* (a review). Nebbadoon, Inc. No date.
   [http://ellis.nebbadoon.com/docs/joined_reviewfiles/CROOKLYN.html]

Epilogue (to *Do the Right Thing*). Spike Lee. English Department.
   University of Pennsylvania. December 17, 1988.
   [www.english.upenn.edu/~afilreis/103/spike-epilogue.html]

Fitzgerald, Sharon. Spike Lee: Fast Forward. *American Visions,* v. 10
   Oct/Nov 1995. p. 20-4+.

Frutkin, Alan. Spike Speaks. *The Advocate.* October 31, 1995.
   [www.advocate.com/html/stories/790/790_spike_int.asp]

Gary, Kelli. Who's Bamboozled? Not Spike Lee. *Film and TV Today.*
   NYU Tisch School of the Arts. Winter, 2001.
   [www.nyu.edu/tisch/filmtv/ftv/filmtv10-5.html]

Geffner, David and Holly Willis. The DV Bamboozle: Ellen Kuras on
   DV's Fatal Flaws. *RES Media.* 2001.
   [www.res.com/spikelee-dv_bamboozle.jsp]

Goldstein, Steve. By Any Means Necessary: Spike Lee on Video's Viability.
   RES Media. 2001.
   [www.res.com/spikelee-by_any_means.jsp]

Harris, Erich Leon. Demystifying Spike Lee. *IndieNetwork.com.* 1998.
   [http://indienetwork.com/moviemaker/features/spikelee.html]

hooks, bell. On Death and Patriarchy. *Zmagazine.* No date.
   [www.lbbs.org/zmag/articles/hooks1.htm]

Jaguar and Spike Lee Team Up for X-Type Advertising. *Motor Trend
   Online.* Auguat 24, 2001.
   [www.motortrend.com/news/stories/010824ja.html]

Jones, Kent. The Invisible Man: Spike Lee. *Film Comment Magazine.*
   July-August 1996.
   [www.archive.filmlinc.com/fcm/1-2-97/spike.htm]

Judell, Brandon. An Interview with Spike Lee, Director of '4 Little Girls.'
   indieWIRE. 2001.
   [www.indiewire.com/film/interviews/int_Lee_Spike_971212.html]

Kamiya, Gary. Backboard Jungle. *Salon.com.* May 1, 1998.
   [www.salon.com/ent/movies/1998/05/cov_01game.html]

Kaufman, Michael T. In a New Film, Spike Lee Tries to do the Right
   Thing. *The New York Times.* Sec. 2, p. 1. June 25, 1989.

Kauffmann, Stanley. Beyond Satire. *The New Republic Online.* October
   30, 2000.
   [www.thenewrepublic.com/103000/kauffmann103000.html]

Kempton, Murray. The Pizza is Burning! *The New York Review of Books.* September 28, 1989.
   [www.nybooks.com/articles/article-preview?article_id=3909]

Knicks, Spike Lee Team Up for Charity Auction. NBA Media Ventures. October 8, 2001.
   [www.nba.com/news/knicks_lee_auction_011008.html?nav=ArticleList]

Lee Opens Up on Career, Upbringing. CNN (with Beverly Schuch). May 11, 1998.
   [www.cnn.com/SHOWBIZ/9805/11/spike.lee/]

Lee, Spike. *Best Seat in the House: A Basketball Memoir.* (excerpt) Random House. No date.
   [www.randomhouse.com/features/spikelee/]

Lee, Spike. Spike Lee: Independent Filmmaker (speech). June 8, 1996. *In Motion Magazine.*
   [www.inmotionmagazine.com/slee.html]

Liz Biz. Urban Legends Reference Pages. August 16, 1999.
   [www.snopes2.com/quotes/claiborn.htm]

Maurer, Monika. *Bamboozled* (a review). *Kamera.co.uk.* 2001.
   [www.kamera.co.uk/reviews_extra/bamboozled.php]

Merida, Kevin. Spike Lee, Holding Court. *Washington Post.* May 1, 1998.
   [www.washingtonpost.com/wp-srv/style/features/lee.htm]

Morgan, David. Wynn Thomas on Filming *Malcolm X. Wide Angle/Close Up.* 2001.
   [http://members.aol.com/morgands3/wynn92.htm]

Nazarinia, Michael. Lee's New Flick 'Bus' Stops Short. *The Daily Bruin* (UCLA). October 16, 1996.
   [www.dailybruin.ucla.edu/db/issues/96/10.16/ae.lee.html]

Nash, Bruce. Spike Lee Films: Box Office Grosses. *The Numbers.* 2001.
   [www.the-numbers.com/people/directors/SLEE.html]

Navy Brass Backs Spike Lee. *NewsMax.com.* July 8, 1999.
   [www.newsmax.com/showinside.shtml?a=1999/7/7/212106]

O'Hehir, Andrew. *Bamboozled. Salon.com.* October 6, 2000.
   [www.salon.com/ent/movies/review/2000/10/06/bamboozled/index.html]

O'Hehir, Andrew. *The Original Kings of Comedy. Salon.com.* August 29, 2000.
   [www.salon.com/ent/movies/review/2000/08/29/kings/index.html]

Pinsker, Sanford. Spike Lee: Protest, Literary Tradition, and the Individual Filmmaker. *Midwest Quarterly.* 1993 (1): 63-76.

Reagan Navy Chief Urges Response to Spike Lee's Comment. *NewsMax.com.* June 23, 1999.
[www.newsmax.com/showinside.shtml?a−1999/6/23/05227]

Rich, Ruby. An Interview with Spike Lee. *Independent View.* No date.
[http://inview.kqed.org/interviews/23/int-win.html]

Ryfle, Steve. Spike Lee: 'Patriot'-Hatin'. *Hollywood.com.* June 6, 2000.
[www.hollywood.com/news/detail/article/312613]

Scambray, Kenneth. *Jungle Fever* (a review). *L'Italio-Americano.* June, 1991.
[http://members.tripod.com/~verdicchio/fever.html]

Schmenner, Will. *Summer of Sam* (a review). *Flak* magazine. 2001.
[www.flakmag.com/film/summerofsam.html

Shaffer, Michael. Lee Spikes Will Smith. *Hollywood.com.* March 19, 2001.
[www.hollywood.com/news/detail/article/313254]

Snow Hill Institute. (homepage) No date.
[http://home.nyc.rr.com/lallan/]

Spike Lee (profile). *The African American Almanac,* 7th ed. Detroit: Gale, 1997.
[www.galegroup.com/free_resources/bhm/bio/lee_s.htm]

Spike Lee Slams Patriot 'Disgrace.' BBC News. July 14, 2000.
[http://news.bbc.co.uk/hi/english/entertainment/newsid_833000/833455.stm]

Spike Lee Takes on Hollywood. *The Sydney Morning Herald.* October 10, 2000.
[www.smh.com.au/news/0010/10/features/features11.html]

Spike Lee. Celebrities. *Hollywood.com.* 2001.
[www.hollywood.com/celebs/bio/celeb/346505]

Spike Lee: Biography and Jointography. *In Motion Magazine.* 1996.
[www.inmotionmagazine.com/slee2.html]

Spike Lee: Filmmaker. *1st Person.* KRT Interactive. No date.
[www.tdo.com/local/graphics/1plee/html/1a.htm]

Spike Lee: The Facts. *E! Online.* 2001.
[www.eonline.com/Facts/People/Bio/0,128,9175,00.html]

Spike Lee's Navy Filming Continued Despite Uproar in Congress. *NewsMax.com.* June 23, 1999.
[www.newsmax.com/showinside.shtml?a=1999/6/23/235124]

Sragow, Michael. Black Like Spike. *Salon.com.* October 26, 2000.
[www.salon.com/ent/col/srag/2000/10/26/spike_lee/]

Sterritt, David. Spike Lee Shocks with Wild Race Tale. *Christian Science Monitor.* October 6, 2000.
[www.csmonitor.com/durable/2000/10/06/fp15s1-csm.shtml]

Stone, Alan A. Spike Lee: Looking Back. *Boston Review.* December 1994/January 1995.
  [http://bostonreview.mit.edu/BR19.6/spike.html]

Susman, Gary. Southern Exposure. *Mr. Showbiz.* 2001.
  [http://mrshowbiz.go.com/celebrities/interviews/291_1.html]

Sylvester, Bruce. One Grain of Sand (review). *Boston Phoenix* CD Reviews. December 15, 1997.
  [www.weeklywire.com/ww/12-15-97/boston_music_clips.html]

Taylor, Charles. Black and White and Taboo All Over. *Salon.com.* February 14, 2000.
  [www.salon.com/ent/feature/2000/02/14/interracial_movies/index.html]

The Morehouse Legacy. Morehouse College. No date.
  [www.morehouse.edu/morehouselegacy/index.html]

Thompson, Andrew. Spike Lee Does the DV Thing. *RES Media.* 2000.

Tuttle, Kate. Lee, Shelton Jackson ('Spike'). *Africana.com.* 2000.
  [www.africana.com/Articles/tt_222.htm]

Williams. Kam. Spike Lee: the 'Bamboozled' Interview. *Black Talent.com.* 2000.
  [http://www.blacktalentnews.com/Spikeleeinterview.html]

Zacharek, Stephanie. David Berkowitz Kvetches About Spike Lee's 'Summer of Sam.' *Salon.com.* June 21, 1999.
  [www.salon.com/ent/log/1999/06/21/berkowitz/]

Bernotas, Bob. *Spike Lee: Filmmaker (People to Know)*. Hillside, NJ: Enslow Publishers, 1993.

Fuchs, Cynthia and Spike Lee. *Spike Lee: Interviews (Conversations With Filmmakers Series)*. Jackson, MS: University Press of Mississippi, 2002.

Haskins, Jim. *Spike Lee: By Any Means Necessary*. New York: Walker, 1997.

Lee, Spike and Lisa Jones. *Uplift the Race: The Construction of School Daze*. New York: Fireside, 1988.

Lee, Spike and Ralph Wiley. *Best Seat in the House: A Basketball Memoir*. New York: Three Rivers Press, 1998.

Lee, Spike et al. *Please, Baby, Please*. New York: Simon & Schuster, 2002.

Lee, Spike. *By Any Means Necessary: The Trials and Tribulations of the Making of Malcolm X*. New York: Hyperion, 1992.

Lee, Spike. *Do the Right Thing: The New Spike Lee Joint*. New York: Simon & Schuster, 1989.

Lee, Spike. *Five for Five: The Films of Spike Lee*. New York: Stewart, Tabori & Chang, 1991.

Lee, Spike. *Mo' Better Blues*. New York: Simon & Schuster, 1990.

Lee, Spike. *Spike Lee's Gotta Have It: Inside Guerrilla Filmmaking*. New York: A Fireside Book Published by Simon & Schuster, Inc., 1987.

McDaniel, Melissa. *Spike Lee: On His Own Terms (Book Report Biography)*. New York: Franklin Watts, 1998.

Akomfrah, John. Spike Lee (interview). *The Guardian.* November 18, 1999.
   [http://film.guardian.co.uk/Guardian_NFT/interview/0,4479,110609,00.html]

Do the Right Thing: A Brief Guide to Spike Lee. *HotWired.* 2001.
   [http://hotwired.lycos.com/popfeatures/96/23/lee.guide.html]

Harris, Erich Leon. Demystifying Spike Lee. *IndieNetwork.com.* 1998.
   [http://indienetwork.com/moviemaker/features/spikelee.html

Jones, Kent. The Invisible Man: Spike Lee. *Film Comment Magazine.*
   July-August 1996.
   [www.archive.filmlinc.com/fcm/1-2-97/spike.htm]

Lee, Spike. Spike Lee: Independent Filmmaker (speech). June 8, 1996.
   In Motion Magazine.
   [www.inmotionmagazine.com/slee.html]

Spike Lee (profile). *The African American Almanac,* 7th ed. Detroit:
   Gale, 1997.
   [www.galegroup.com/free_resources/bhm/bio/lee_s.htm]

Academy Award nominations
  for *Do the Right Thing,* 40
  for *4 Little Girls,* 67
Aiello, Danny, in *Do the Right Thing,*
  38
Ali, Mohammed, 88
Allen, Ray, in *He Got Game,* 68
Answer, The, 27

Baldwin, James, 10
Bamboozled, 7-8, 9-10, 12, 71, 88
  cast of, 7, 10
  and racism, 7-8, 9-10, 12-15
  reviews of, 8, 9, 13
  story of, 8, 10
  title for, 15
Baraka, Amiri, 52-53
Bassett, Angela, in *Malcolm X,* 54
Berkowitz, David, 23, 70
Bertolucci, Bernardo, 23
Birth of a Nation, 25-27
Black New Wave, 31
Bythewood, Reggie Rock, and *Get
  On the Bus,* 64

Canton, Mark, 83
Cedric the Entertainer, in *The Original
  Kings of Comedy,* 71
Cimino, Michael, 23
Claiborne-Winfrey "feud," 44-45
Clockers, 63-64, 78
Cochran, Johnnie, 64
Columbia Pictures, and *School Daze,*
  35
Cosby, Bill, 56
Crooklyn, 19, 62-63

Davidson, Tommy, in *Bamboozled,* 10
Deer Hunter, The, 23
Disney, and *Summer of Sam,* 70
Do the Right Thing, 15, 37-41, 43, 62,
  76, 77, 86
  and awards, 40
  cast for, 37
  and racism, 37-41
  reviews of, 38, 39-40
  score for, 38

story of, 37-39
success of, 40
and Universal, 8-9

Emmy nominations, for *4 Little Girls,*
  67
Esposito, Giancarlo, 35
Esquire magazine, 44-45

Farrakhan, Louis, 53-54, 64
Fishburne, Laurence, 35
Forty Acres and a Mule Filmmaking,
  30-31, 71
Forty Acres and a Mule Institute,
  29-30
40 Acres and Mule, 71
4 Little Girls (TV), 66-67
Freeman, Al, Jr., in *Malcolm X,* 54

Get On the Bus, 64-66
Gibson, Mel, 81
Girl 6, 64
Glover, Savion, in *Bamboozled,* 10
Griffith, D.W., 25-27
Griffith, Michael, 37

Hall, Albert, in *Malcolm X,* 54
Harris, Zelda, in *Crooklyn,* 62
Harvard University, 8
Harvey, Steve, in *The Original Kings
  of Comedy,* 71
Hawkins, Yusuf, 47-48
He Got Game, 67-68, 78
Heston, Charlton, 81
Huey P. Newton Story, A, 71, 73
Hughley, D.L., in *The Original Kings
  of Comedy,* 71

Island Pictures
  and *School Daze,* 35
  and *She's Gotta Have It,* 29

Jarmusch, Jim, 27
*Joe's Bed-Stuy Barbershop: We Cut
  Heads,* 27
John Dewey High School, 20
Jordan, Michael, 88

Jungle Fever, 47-49, 52, 67
    cast for, 47
    reviews of, 48-49
    and stereotypes, 48
    story of, 47-48

Kamiya, Gary, 78
Kauffman, Stanley, 14-15
Kempton, Murray, 38
King, Martin Luther, Jr., and *Do the*
    Right Thing, 38, 39
Kuras, Ellen, 88
Kurosawa, Akira, 23

Last Hustle in Brooklyn, 23-24
Lee, Bill (father), 18-19, 20, 38, 46
Lee, Cinque (sister), 18
    and *Crooklyn,* 62
Lee, Jacqueline (mother), 19, 23
Lee, Joie Susannah (sister), 18
    and *Crooklyn,* 62
Lee, Linette Lewis (wife), 63, 67
Lee, Satchel (daughter), 89
Lee, Spike
    and awards, 27, 28, 29, 40, 67
    birth of, 18
    and bodyguards, 53
    childhood of, 17-20, 23
    children of, 89
    and controversy, 8-9, 13-15, 44-45,
        46-48, 75-83
    and decision to be director, 23
    and digital video, 87-88
    and early films, 23-24, 27, 28-29
    education of, 19, 20-27
    and *Esquire* magazine interview,
        44-45
    family of, 18-20
    and Fort Greene, 17-20, 30-31
    and gatekeepers, 13-14, 87
    goals of, 88-89
    and gun violence, 81
    and homosexuality, 78-81
    and marriage, 63, 67
    in New York City, 17-20, 23,
        86-87
    and *The Patriot,* 81

    as professor, 8
    and role in films, 35, 37, 54
    and Will Smith, 81
    and Spike as nickname, 18
    style of, 8-9, 34-35, 37, 46, 58,
        66, 88
    and views on filmmaking, 85-89
    and young filmmakers, 87-88
Legend of Bagger Vance, The, 81
Lindo, Delroy, in *Crooklyn,* 62
Los Angeles Film Critics Association's
    Best Director award, for *Do the*
    Right Thing, 40

Mac, Bernie, in *The Original Kings*
    of Comedy, 71
Malcolm X, 49
    and *Bamboozled,* 15
    and *Do the Right Thing,* 38, 39
    See also Malcolm X
Malcolm X, 15, 40, 49-59, 61
    budget for, 52, 54-57
    cast for, 45, 53, 54
    locations for, 57
    and objections to Lee as director,
        52-53
    and promotional merchandise, 58
    reviews of, 58-59
    screenplay for, 53
    shooting of, 53-54
    story of, 54
    and Warner Brothers, 52, 54-57
Marsalis, Branford, 88
Maslin, Janet, 68
Mays, Willie, 88
Messenger, The, 28-29, 35
Million Man March, 64
Mo' Better Blues, 45-47
    cast for, 45-46, 53
    reviews of, 46-47
    score for, 46
    and stereotypes, 46-47
    story of, 45-46
Morehouse College, 20-24
Motion Picture Arts and Sciences'
    Student Academy Award, for
    Bed-Stuy, 27, 28

Nation of Islam
  Lee's bodyguards from, 53-54
  and Million Man March, 64
Newton, Huey, 71, 73
New York University, 8, 24-27

Original Kings of Comedy, The, 71

Phifer, Mekhi, in *Clockers,* 63-64
Pollock, Tom, 9
Price, Richard, 63
Prix de Jeunesse Award, for *She's Gotta Have It,* 29

Reardon, Barry, 57
Rich, Matty, 43-44
Roth, Joe, 70

St. Ann's school, 19
Schickel, Richard, 64
School Daze, 33-37, 80
  budget for, 35
  and Columbia Pictures, 35
  and guerrilla filmmaking techniques, 34-35
  and racism, 34-35, 37
  reviews of, 35-37
  story of, 35
Sciorra, Annabella, in *Jungle Fever,* 47
Scorsese, Martin, 23
She's Gotta Have It, 29-31, 76-77
  and awards, 29
  budget for, 29, 57

and Island Pictures, 29
  shooting of, 29
  story of, 29, 34, 62, 76-77
  success of, 29-31, 33, 34
Singleton, John, 43-44, 76
Smith, Roger Guenveur, 71, 73
Smith, Will
  Get on the Bus financed by, 64
  and *The Legend of Bagger Vance,* 81
Snipes, Wesley
  Get on the Bus financed by, 64
  in *Jungle Fever,* 47
Sterritt, David, 9
Stone, Alan, 36-37, 46-47, 82
Stranger than Paradise, 27
Summer of Sam, 68, 70-71

Taylor, Charles, 48-49
Thompson, Andrew, 13

Universal, and *Do the Right Thing,* 8-9

Warner Brothers, 83
  and *Clockers,* 63
  and *Malcolm X,* 52, 54-57
Washington, Denzel
  in *He Got Game,* 68
  in *Malcolm X,* 45, 53
  in *Mo' Better Blues,* 45-46, 53
Wayans, Damon, in *Bamboozled,* 7, 10
West, Cornel, 59
William Morris agency, 28
Woodard, Alfre, in *Crooklyn,* 62

About the Author

Charles J. Shields is the author of 12 books for Chelsea House. Before turning to writing fulltime, he was chairman of the English department at Homewood-Flossmoor High School in Flossmoor, Illinois. His 1985 book, The College Guide for Parents (The College Board) won an award from the Educational Press Association. He has degrees in English and history from the University of Illinois, Urbana-Champaign. Shields lives in Homewood, Illinois with his wife, Guadalupe, an educational consultant in reading and literacy to the Chicago Public Schools.